Credo

Credo

Louis Evely

Translated by Rosemary Sheed

Fides Publishers, Inc.
Notre Dame, Indiana

First published 1967
Sheed & Ward Ltd, 33 Maiden Lane, London WC2, and
Sheed & Ward Pty Ltd, 28 Bourke Street, Melbourne

AMERICAN EDITION 1967
By special arrangement with Sheed & Ward, London.

Nihil Obstat: Louis J. Putz, C.S.C.
               University of Notre Dame

Imprimatur: Leo A. Pursley, D.D.
              Bishop of Fort Wayne-South Bend

The Nihil Obstat and Imprimatur are a declaration that
a book is considered to be free from doctrinal
or moral error. It is not implied that those who have
granted the Nihil Obstat and Imprimatur agree with the
contents, opinions, or statements expressed.

Manufactured in the U.S.A.

Contents

1
The creed

Does one ever pray the creed—ever say it as a personal prayer, choosing it rather than another prayer because one enjoys saying it? Does one even think of it as a prayer? It is, in fact, the prayer of our baptism, our confirmation, and our dying moments: 'Go forth, O christian soul, in the name of the Father who created thee, the Son who suffered for thee, the Holy Spirit whom thou hast received within thee . . .'

We have of course recited it hundreds of times. We have proclaimed it. It is a profession of faith whereby we declare what we believe; and so it should be. But if it is no more than this, it would seem that its only value to us lies in enabling us to assert ourselves. It is just another way of talking about ourselves—*my* faith, *my* creed, *my* response, *my* fidelity to the Lord.

So many of our prayers are given a twist to satisfy our individualism—we are adept at making this kind of use of any material that comes to hand. And for this purpose the creed is not really a prayer at all—'It doesn't say anything about me!' Now the Hail Mary brings us back into the picture: the beginning is somewhat irrelevant with its formal preamble; 'The Lord is with thee'—after all, she already knows that. It needs no stressing. But a moment's patience brings us to the 'personal' part, to the real prayer: 'Pray for us sinners . . .' That's us. We can wake up and begin to take part; this is, after all, where the congregation joins in.

Similarly with the Our Father. We wait while the priest recites the opening phrases: 'Hallowed be thy name'; we listen in silence. 'Thy kingdom come'; we remain silent. 'Thy will be done . . .'; there is nothing for us to say. But when it comes to 'Give us this day our daily bread . . .' there is a stirring among the flock. This is where we come in; now it begins to be interesting. And even when we say the whole prayer to ourselves alone is it exactly the same; there is the same vacuous passivity at the beginning, the same maudlin interest at the end.

We are all too ready to believe that our 'personal' prayers are the most genuine. Or rather, we are mistaken in thinking that our indvidual, private prayer—'alone with God'—is the only way of entering 'personally' into contact with our Lord. Such prayer is in fact more often than not simply a cover-up for our self-centredness, and hence an introversion rather than a communication, a closing rather than an opening.

The sense of loneliness is the awareness of

2

everything in us that is not yet open to the Spirit, still heavy, immovable, turned inwards. If people did but realise it when they try to pray to console their loneliness, the answer to such prayer lies in leaving solitude behind, in sacrificing it to God and to their fellow men, in restoring their powers of communication. The magnificent objectiveness of the creed lifts us out of our bog of sentimentality.

Here, at last, we are concerned wholly with God and not with ourselves. It is a prayer of praise, of expansion, of thanksgiving, or eucharist, of pure rejoicing. For preference it should be sung rather than said, and sung with others rather than alone. It is a contemplative prayer. In it we watch the slow unfolding of the history of God—God's initiatives, what God does, what he is. And we join ourselves to him. Surely we can be far more sure that we are genuinely praying when our thought is directed thus, than when we are analysing, examining, and expressing ourselves.

The best definition of a bore is 'a man who keeps talking about himself when I want to tell him about me'. Do we perhaps secretly find that the prayers that talk 'only' about God are a bit of a bore? God can only set us free from ourselves if we listen to him, praise him, glorify him, and thank him. He wills to raise us above the level of our own complaints and resentments, but we make so much noise that he cannot get through to us. Genuine prayer is nothing other than a getting-out-of-oneself, a focusing of interest away from oneself upon another—upon a person. God is someone who breaks into our life and calls us by our name; and he reveals his name to us so that we will do the same to him. Throughout the bible he tells us things about himself. He speaks to us in a completely open-hearted way as one person to another, and invites us to speak to him in the same way.

In the creed, we speak of God, we contemplate him, we marvel at him. The creed is a kind of detailed explanation of the magnificat: 'He that is mighty hath done great things to me.' Listen to some of its phrases: Creator of heaven and earth ... his only Son ... who suffered under Pontius Pilate ... rose again ... I believe in the Holy Ghost ... How different—and what a revealing difference it is—is the concrete, historical creed, the community's hymn of the history of salvation, from our individualistic, abstract, pretentious ('I believe all'), and *empty* 'act of faith'. Up to the seventeenth century, the christian act of faith *was* the creed.

Nowhere does the creed advert to what we do or could do 'for God'. It is the summing up of genuine religion. There is a false religion (to which many of us subscribe), a religion of the things I do for God; and it is a dreary, whining, miserable religion, just as the things I do for God are poor, dreary, whining, and miserable. It is a religion we can easily have too much of; since we do not want to do more, we do not want to know more either. It is a religion on the same scale as ourselves, the religion of what man can devise to try to reach an inaccessible God, to win over a reluctant God.

4

But the other—the true—religion is the religion of the great things God has done for us; it calls for no imagination on our part, for God himself who continually creates and strengthens the bond between God and man; that it is he who calls us, not we who call him; and that throughout history (the creed covers all of the history of this world and the next, from the creation to eternal life) it is God who declares himself, shows himself, and makes himself known to us. It is God who has invented the miracles of salvation—incarnation, redemption, church, sacraments, saints.

The creed brings home to us the riches of God and his gift to us. It is an exciting religion that makes us want to know more. Religion is transformed from a series of obligations to a series of liberations: how wonderful to be no longer crushed beneath my own helplessness and guilt! How wonderful that God has taken me to himself and come to my help! Our faith means that God loves man, not that man is obliged to love God. What a sense of security and comfort we get when we finally come to believe that our salvation rests in his hands.

The creed is trinitarian in structure, following the same pattern as the Glory be to the Father, though developed in a more complicated way. It is trinitarian not only because it celebrates the names and the works of the first, second, and third divine persons, because it sets forth the mystery of the Trinity. It is primarily so because it makes us participate in that mystery by the direction and impetus it gives our prayer: it absorbs us in someone else, draws us out of ourselves—just as God, being one in three, is forever delighting in another. Like the life of the Trinity, the creed really prayed is an ec-stasy, a complete 'standing out of oneself' to give one's attention to someone else. The Trinity is the mystery of that going out of oneself.

The Trinity—the mystery of the holy Trinity—is the expression of that amazing truth that God *is* love, and is only love. To realise that God is three is to realise that life, for God, consists in loving himself better in another ('This is my beloved Son, with whom I am well pleased', Mt 3: 17), in referring to another ('the Son can do nothing of his own accord, but only what he sees the Father doing', Jn 5:19; 'as I hear, I judge', Jn 5: 30; 'the Father is greater than I', Jn 14:28), bearing witness to another ('the Spirit of truth . . . will bear witness to me', Jn 15:26).

The distinction of persons in the Trinity is based on their roles in giving: they are three, who live to give, and they give themselves so totally that they are nevertheless one. The Father only expresses himself by uttering the Son. The Son is wholly a gift of himself to the Father—a giving back, a eucharist. The Spirit is wholly the witness to the Father and the Son:

> He will not speak on his own authority, but whatever he hears he will speak, . . . he will take what is mine . . . All that the Father has is mine; therefore I said that he will take what is mine and declare it to you. [Jn 15:13–15.]

6

We have to 'get out of ourselves' in order to love anyone. The divine persons' whole existence is a 'getting out of themselves'. It costs us great effort to reach the point of sharing out treasures, of resolving to enjoy together things we could keep to ourselves. The divine persons exist only by being several together. We can see a kind of analogy to this in families, or other communities where there is love: one is more oneself with others than alone. And one can hope to become ever more the person one is meant to be by learning to love ever more deeply, to express oneself, communicate, confide, discover oneself—in others and with others.

The divine persons do everything together, and all each one's joy comes from what the others do. 'Not in the singleness of one person', not in loneliness, we exclaim in the preface of the Trinity, rejoicing that God is not solitary, but exists in several persons, exists in loving. Let us hope that God, being total self-giving, can teach us, too, that the only joy is to love. The Trinity makes it possible for us to understand that God is the spirit of love, and that to love is to be in God. 'He who loves is born of God and knows God' (1 Jn 4 : 7)—because he is like God.

Our whole life will be governed, consciously or unconsciously, by the idea we have of the Trinity. It was Adam's idea of the Trinity—of the life of God—that led to mankind's taking the direction it did. It was to be 'like God' that he wanted to free himself of the need to obey, to trust, to depend on someone else, to be content not to know everything. It is worth asking ourselves whether our dream is also to become stronger, more self-sufficient, better able to look after ourselves, independent, free, and alone—or more and more dependent, loving, involved with others, vulnerable to others, unable to get along without others. For we shall become the God we believe in. If we think of God as autonomous, rich, subject to no one, free of all constraint, then we shall logically make every effort to become the same. But once we really *believe* that God is love—in other words attachment, tenderness, obedience, self-giving, communion, longing, waiting—then we also, like Adam and all mankind, wanting to 'become as God', will rejoice whenever we find ourselves dependent, attached, subject to our own affectionate feelings, unable to be happy alone.

The creed, by drawing us out of ourselves to talk to us about someone else, to rejoice in Another, is a direct drinking at the spring of divine life. We shall have understood all that we need to understand of the Trinity when, having 'got out of ourselves', we can say the creed with such joy, such delight in the great things God has done, that we no longer even notice that we aren't talking about ourselves, that we no longer even want to say anything about ourselves beyond proclaiming our wonder and gratitude. Our joy, then, will be one with the Son's: 'O righteous Father, the world has not known thee, but I have known thee . . .' (Jn 17:25); 'I thank thee, Father, Lord of heaven and earth, . . .' (Mt 11:25).

The canon of the mass talks of the 'sacrifice of

8

praise'. The creed is a sacrifice of praise. It teaches us not to believe in what we are, in what we feel, in what we do, in what we want or what we deserve, but rather in what God does, wills, and gives.

But, you may object, the creed begins all the same with the word 'I'. No, not really. It begins with the phrase 'I believe'; and the 'believe' is an immediate handing back, so to say, of the 'I', cancelling it out, or, if you like, setting it free. There is an immediate getting out of oneself to enter the world of another. The 'I' is awoken only to be contradicted, for belief means leaving oneself to enter God. And entering God is not a conquest, but a renunciation; it makes one available, opens up one's barriers, places one in his hands. To say 'I believe' is the same as saying 'I place my trust, I no longer want to argue or defend my position, I hand myself over'. Entering God is to enter a state of poverty. To make an act of faith is to make an act of poverty. Poverty is the first of the beatitudes precisely because it is a response, because it corresponds to the opening of the creed: 'I believe'.

'Blessed are the poor in spirit, for theirs is the kingdom of heaven [in which we declare our faith in the creed]' (Mt 5:3). Only the poor man can know God, for only he can get out of himself. Poverty is not a vow, a counsel of perfection, a crown of the spiritual life as we are accustomed to think. It is a point of departure. If you refuse to be poor, then you fail the entrance exam, the beginning of the creed.

For the beatitudes have this in common with the creed, that they speak of God, they describe divine behaviour, they tell us God's preferences. It is significant that christian education so often begins not with the beatitudes, but with the ten commandments, most of which are negative. The commandments talk about us, our obligations, what we must do, and what we must do without, 'for God'. We can govern our lives by the commandments, guarantee a clear conscience by keeping them (thus holding God at arm's length). If you want to keep out of trouble with a superior, keep the rules, and then he will have no hold over you. In that way we can acquire self-sufficiency and independence. We can manage quite well without God's pardon by simply keeping the ten commandments.

But the beatitudes are different. They tell us what God is like, and how we can be like him. You can't feel smugly that you are 'keeping' the beatitudes. Only by a special miracle can we even *want* to live them.

Faith is an act, the act of the poor man, of the man who no longer sets any store by himself. To accept to enter the creed is to accept to be despoiled of everything one has. But what has one? A lot that means far more to us than just our money: our cares, our sufferings, our problems, our griefs. The rich young man who went away sad 'because he had great possessions' was, equally with the miser, refusing to say the creed, refusing to enter into the joy of the creed, preferring to talk of himself, to remain alone with his

10

sufferings, his worries, his problems—important problems, of course, bearing on the salvation of the world. Conscious of his responsibilities he makes a retreat to help fulfil them, to meditate, to work out solutions, christian solutions. And the answer he gets is: Sing the creed; learn how to sing the creed lustily with everyone else. He has concrete, important, urgent problems, decisions to make involving a great many other people—and he is told simply: 'Stop thinking of yourself. Sing: "I believe in God, the Father almighty ... was conceived, ... born, ... and rose again ..."' And he goes away sorrowful with his great possessions, his great questions, his great worries and concerns. He was already fully occupied—with himself.

Why do we cling so to our troubles? We seem to enjoy being overburdened, as though our adversities were a warm garment we feared to take off. 'It had to happen, my luck is always bad.' For some reasons we find that easier to say than 'He that is mighty has done great things for me'. Why do we thus hang back in the face of happiness? What exactly do we fear to lose?

Melancholy is the final form of selfishness, and the most tenacious of all. One can have a certain independence in one's gloom: 'Things couldn't be worse', we can say, taking satisfaction from our hopelessness. To lay oneself open to hope is to be prepared to be dependent, to expect, to undergo changes, to be turned upside down. 'My Father is working still' (Jn 5:17): to set foot in the world of hope, love, and joy—the world of the beatitudes, of poverty and faith—is to be constantly urged to go further. 'Was conceived by the Holy Ghost, born . . . died . . . rose again . . .' Blessed are the poor, for they are sufficiently detached from their own miseries to consent to enter this movement of joy, to find happiness through someone else.

Another form of 'riches' that will prevent our singing the creed all together, and which we absolutely must rid ourselves of, is class prejudice. Nothing could be more opposed to the movement of love, enthusiasm, and communion that the creed should stimulate in us, for it erects walls of ignorance and hostility between us and other people. We can be equally paralysed by a sense of superiority and one of inferiority—paralysed, and paralysing. The man who thinks himself better than me will paralyse me by his well-bred patronage. But the one who thinks himself beneath me, and makes a point of behaving distantly and sulkily for fear of a snub, blocks up the possibility of communion just as effectively. Some people shrivel you up; others, already shrivelled themselves, start off by being surly so as to be able at least to have the honour of being the first to be unpleasant. To behave unlikably prevents the hurt of feeling disliked. But it is as serious a sin as failing to love others, for it is a 'scandal', something that helps others to sin.

It all springs from an acceptance, from whatever angle one sees it, of the tyranny of social class, from agreeing to enter this play-acting of completely unchristian social strata. Some people think it can be overcome by reversing the ladder

—but that is merely a change of riches, a change of pharisaism.

The old-style pharisee says: 'How thankful I am that I am not like those ill-bred publicans; I come from a nice family; I am honourable, disciplined, hard-working, honest. How thankful I am that my children are in good schools, their youthful innocence preserved; I am inculcating in them a sense of effort, of dignity, and so on, and so forth.' That particular pharisee is a bit old-fashioned. He doesn't realise that all his ideas have been classed—pigeon-holed—as 'wrong' by really up-to-date christians. What they want is the publican's place right at the back, well behind the pillar. They gloss over any distinguished people in their family who might compromise their abjection, and from their pew by the holy-water stoup they give thanks to the Lord: 'How thankful I am not to be one of those upper-class pharisees. Luckily I don't come from a good family, so I can despise them with a free mind. For I am a poor man; my poverty is guaranteed, so I am certain to get a good place in heaven. Don't anyone ask me to change or make friends with the middle-class. My publican's halo has cost me a lot; I have paid through the nose for my poverty!'

The modern publicans are as proud of themselves as the pharisees of old. Their poverty is really nothing but a new wealth, an acquisition. We are all rich, hideously rich; wealth is not the things we possess, but the things that possess us.

No one is master of his weatlh, but its servant: and no one can serve two masters.

The wealth that is accursed is the possession that enslaves us instead of setting us free. And we are all held, kept back, bound, fettered, imprisoned by our class prejudice. The awkwardness, the inability to make contact, the failure to be natural—all the barriers to our relationship with others—do they not all result from our training, with its respect for categories, a fear of doing anything 'not done'?

Which of us dares to by-pass all this and greet absolutely *anyone* as a true brother? For that is what brotherhood means. Absolutely anyone— a 'big' man or a small. Not many will carry poverty to the point of leaving all thoughts of class behind, whether they come from the top or bottom—and to leave *either* means poverty, means becoming disestablished if you like. It is as mortifying to give up despising the rich as to give up 'doing good' to the poor.

The final form of riches I want to condemn here, from which we must detach ourselves, is our ideas of God. God is not an idea, nor a system of ideas. He is not something, but someone. We must believe—in God. The truly poor man is so attentive to God that God can reveal himself to him from day to day. For him God is always new, because he is alive. Life involves change. In a living organism the cells never stop coming to be, growing, dying, starting again. To imprison God in a permanent formula is to deny that he is life. 'Because I live, you will live also' (Jn 14:19). But

14

'the world knew him not' (Jn 1:9): the world knows only formulas—catechism answers, definitions. There are definitions a-plenty to classify and catalogue him once for all.

Time and again I have heard some such thing as this from students of mine: 'My parents are wonderful—young, modern, active. They have read everything, and really know what is going on. But when it comes to religion, they are completely stick-in-the-mud; you can't ask them anything or discuss anything. Religion is something you just accept—you can't talk about it. When it comes to that they are completely out of date.' And I have met some of these parents. I have told them what their children think, and some of their responses have been truly frightening. One mother was a 'splendid catholic', from a traditionally catholic family; her son had lost his faith, but she obviously hadn't lost hers. Her faith was her anchor. When I asked her, 'Why don't you talk to your son? Why won't you discuss it with him', she replied: 'But Father, if you begin to examine things too closely, where will it end?' Did she really think that a sincere examination of what she believed, undertaken to enlighten her son, would really do harm? She certainly believed that she believed in God! Yet what unbelief must underlie such a refusal to speak, how little trust in God to feel she could raise no question about him. Her son said to me: 'I have worn out my brother's clothes, and my parents' religion.' Yet what else could he possibly do with a religion like that?

His parents' religion was just such a garment,

a family cast-off to be worn without the slightest alteration. And she thought she had the faith. She was a catholic of the old school; no one in her family ever talked about such things, no questions were ever asked; for questioning would be sinful. To them the virtue of faith meant precisely asking no questions, leaving well alone. Faith of this kind is of course not faith at all, but a terrible incredulity, a terrible fear that if you question anything the whole edifice will crumble. It is a treasure to be kept as carefully as all life's other treasures; a fear of losing what you have got, a refusal to move from the position in which you are entrenched, a miserly clutching at truth—or at what you think is truth. But touch it, and it won't be true any more, for it is dead and empty, like a hollow tree which stands only so long as there is no wind.

To know God one must be poor; one must expunge all one's own ideas, open one's mind wide and say 'I believe'—and then wait. To say 'I believe' is to ask a question; it is to offer God an emptiness to fill, knowing with total certainty that he will fill it. It means ceasing to depend on our own reasoning, our own judgement, on the autonomy which would let us believe only what we can prove conclusively. When you have presented a watertight proof of the existence of God, after all, do you believe in God? or do you merely believe in your proof?

This is the renunciation that Adam could not make; he should have had faith—in regard to a tree. Adam should have trusted, and should have rejected the fruit that was to make him 'know' more. He should have accepted the poverty of not knowing quite everything in his happiness. But that he could not bear. He wanted to taste, to experiment, to prove everything, to be in control. He could not stop worrying and place his trust in another. He sought further illumination of the light that was his joy, and so lost it altogether. He was then plunged into darkness, the darkness St John describes as being inimical to the light. He could no longer see God, nor understand the things of God, for such understanding is given only to the poor. Blessed are the poor, for theirs is the kingdom of heaven:

I thank thee, Father, Lord of Heaven and earth, that thou hast hidden these things from the wise and understanding and revealed them to babes. [Mt 11:25; Lk 10:21.]

The true sign that we have God's life in us is that the things of God have become ours, so that we respond to them with interest, excitement, enthusiasm, and are never weary of talking about them. The creed is the song of wonder of the poor man who has been filled with good things, the magnificat of all redeemed creation. Like the magnificat, the creed is also the hymn of those who align themselves with God, knowing his ways and rejoicing in them, happy to suffer together with him (as in the beatitudes). 'He suffered under Pontius Pilate, was crucified, died, and was buried' —that is how God's marvellous plan unfolds. 'Blessed are the poor . . . , those who mourn . . . , those who are persecuted'—all these are God's ways: to suffer, to die, to be buried. This is how God acts; and if you too suffer and die and are buried, you can rejoice. Your feet are on the right path; you are on the road to the kingdom.

Events crowd in upon us, disturbing our calm, plunging us into the mainstream of God's life. We must not shiver on the bank, but dive in. Every vocation is in the terms St Peter heard:

> When you were young, you girded yourself and walked where you would; but when you are old, you will stretch out your hands, and another will gird you and carry you where you do not wish to go. [Jn 21 : 18.]

Marriage does this just as the priesthood does. It is an act of faith, a departure: 'Therefore a man leaves his father and his mother and cleaves to his wife' (Gen 2 : 24; cf. Mk 10 : 7). In other words, don't stay comfortably settled in with your parents (or parents-in-law!). Risk all; set forth!

A retreat is a setting forth. In it we run a terrible risk—the risk of believing, of loving, of setting out on the road. It is God's way always to send us. Mary Magdalen wanted to cling to the knees of the risen Christ, but was told 'Go to my brethren' (Jn 20 : 17). The disciples at Emmaus, as soon as they recognised our Lord, knew that they must leave this place where they felt such joy to go out and bear witness. When St Peter protested his love to Christ ('Simon, son of John, do you love me?' 'Yes, Lord; you know that I love you'), he was told at once, 'Feed my sheep' (Jn 21 : 26, 17).

Go. Get to work. Join the others. You will be hurled out—out of your habits, your comfort, your social class, out of yourself. We too must make our pasch, our Passover from this world to the Father.

2
I believe

Faith is a despoliation, for it means becoming like him whose joy is to be poor and to give all. Only to the poor can God communicate himself, for they alone are like him in this. To believe means first of all to assent to the beatitudes.

Faith is not something we possess, but rather something that dispossesses us. To use religion to make ourselves feel comfortable or important is a complete sham. To have a ready-made religion handed on to us by someone else and accept it without wanting to examine it—this is not faith, but unbelief. To believe in God is to believe in someone who will always be far beyond us, who will for ever be presenting a new aspect of himself to us. Faith is not an acquisition, but a call; not a security, but a risk; not a consolation, but an adventure. Faith is not resting in a haven, but being open to every activity and danger.

How terrible was the trial Christ's contemporaries had to undergo. Those Jews, like us, thought they believed: they believed in their religion and its priests, in their parents and their religious education. Then, suddenly, God was in their midst, and they did not believe in God.

We all know people who have believed for so long that they do not believe any more, who have been waiting for so long that they no longer expect anything. They have put dogmas in place of faith, formulae in place of life, ceremonial in place of truth. Do they believe in God, or only in the people who have told them about him? 'You are lucky to be able to believe', say kindly unbelievers. To believe means to put oneself at God's disposal. And no one hears the word of God without being summoned by it—to go. 'Leave everything . . .' We shall be Abraham's sons when we really set out to leave all our hiding places, even the religious ones (the prayers that move us so deeply, the sacraments that have become magic, the empty, 'consoling' services), to abandon all the manifold activities that preserve us from really having to believe. But while faith calls for this despoliation, this detachment, this self-renunciation, it is equally true that it is also the most natural, most joyful, most truly alive movement possible. It has been said that 'faith is inherent in the soul, but the soul never stops struggling against it'.

Nothing is better, nothing more pleasant, than to trust someone—to place oneself totally in the hands of someone else. For to do so is totally *filial*. Faith is the attitude of a son, and we are made to be sons and daughters. To be completely independent, to trust no one, is stifling; the attitude of unbelief is an exhausting one to maintain. Faith is far more natural than what we are accustomed to think of as our nature. Behind all our struggles for freedom lies a crying need to trust, to submit as sons to a father. We are infinitely more believing than we think, more filial than we begin to realise. Sons by the very fact of having been created, we are doubly so when we have been baptised. When Christ spoke of his Father, when (in St John's gospel) he revealed the most wonderful secrets of his relationship as son, he said:

He who sent me is with me; he has not left me alone, for I always do what is pleasing to him. [Jn 8:29.]

The Son can do nothing of his own accord, but only what he sees the Father doing; for whatever he does, that the Son does likewise. For the Father loves the Son, and shows him all that he himself is doing. [Jn 5:19f.]

'As he spoke thus', says St John, 'many believed in him' (Jn 8:30).

Hearing our Lord speak of his Father like this makes us suddenly feel like orphans. For all of us were created for just such a happy, close, grateful relationship, yet we never attain it. We have been cripples, disabled, with that most terrible of all disabilities—the one we are so unaware of that we take it for a healthy state. We did not even realise that we lacked a father; we were made to be sons, yet all our efforts have been towards emancipation and rebellion. Everyone who heard the Son speak of his relationship with the Father heard for the first time something completely natural, someone speaking as they had never been able to do, and this stirred them deeply. Each suddenly felt a lack, and a call. To be with the Son is to become what we are made to be: sons, brothers, children. It is to become again 'like one of these little ones', to reawaken to simplicity, to trust, to faith—to begin, in short, to enter the kingdom.

Faith is the natural energiser of the mind. There must be some kind of faith before one can even ask a question. A wise priest once said that to ask a question is an act of faith, because it means believing that there is an answer. Asking questions is an act of faith, and it is childlike. Children ask more questions than anyone else because they are more filial, more poor. They are full of faith. It is quite frightening how sure they are that we can explain everything to them, how trusting they are, expecting so much from us. To keep asking questions is to display a child's faith; it is natural, it is filial, to believe that there will be an answer, that the world is intelligible, that there is a point at which truth and goodness are one. But believing means being prepared to wait. Faith requires endless patience, endless and unwearying trust.

Patiently asking questions, affirming one's conviction that the world is intelligible, is an expression of faith in an intelligent Creator. It means, too, loving that Creator enough to believe that he wants to see us come to an understanding of his creation. It is important to realise this.

When scholars look for the reasons of things they cannot explain, they are making an act of faith in the intelligibility of the world. Every laboratory is a place of faith. In Mendelier's table of the ninety-two simple bodies there were for a long time some irregularities. In this marvellous and all-but perfect pattern of curves, there were two or three blanks. This table, with its pattern of simple bodies given in order of increasing atomic weight, and its regular curves, still had some faults. The scientists knew, without a shadow of doubt, that the missing bodies existed. They sought, they waited, they hoped—and finally they found them. They knew that, such a mathematical harmony *must* be perfect. Their faith in a well-constructed mathematical universe was total.

But when it comes to the moral sphere, or the religious sphere; when what is at stake is the most vital thing of all; when it is a question of whether our life has a meaning, whether our existence has any use, whether the God who invented electricity and sound waves, loves us, where we came from, where we are going to (and whether it is worth the effort of getting there); when it comes to all these central matters, then the smallest difficulty or setback drives us to distraction, despair, hopeless resignation. Any accident, any suffering, any unusual gloom, and the world stops. That is the end. It is hopeless. We shall never understand. If there were a God, such things would not happen.

As regards our own lives, we suddenly abandon all thoughts of possible intelligibility. We stop being scholarly or scientific; in other words, we stop asking questions and believing that there are answers. We are resigned to being 'senseless'—without meaning, without direction, without orientation—as soon as our own destiny is in question.

But are you sure that your life (this unhappiness, this misfortune, this accident)—are you sure that it is what you think? that it is no more than what you see? Surely even today things do not look the same as they did yesterday. And perhaps there are other points of view from which these events would look quite different, and mean something else. Wouldn't it be wiser to wait before committing yourself? Couldn't you have believed it to be intelligible, and therefore hoped one day to understand it? Couldn't you have had patience? Couldn't you have had faith? Our faith is fitful, short-sighted, easily discouraged, quick to despair, to give in.

We have our emotional moments—a beautiful Mass, a star-spangled sky, a moment of pure music, the rediscovery of a favourite poet, a breathtaking view: we are suddenly caught up, moved to faith, hope, and love once more. It may last for an hour or two, then down we slip again. We have our helps—perhaps a certain book, or writer, or record, or landscape—which can be trusted to bring us back, if we run to them, to enable us to begin again to believe, to commit ourselves, to be happy, to trust, to see some sense and direction in our lives. But we lack even the courage to make use of them; we haven't even enough faith to call for help. We become so overwhelmed by our unbelief that it even prevents us from going to the spot where we know we shall find renewed strength and hope. (Just as there are evenings when one feels too exhausted to make the effort of going to bed.) The faith of most of us is in some such state as this.

From time to time, however, we escape. The most disenchanted and discouraged christian occasionally makes the effort to go to a cinema, a theatre, a concert. This surely is in hopes of finding a world in which events have a meaning, sounds have a meaning, words have a meaning— in hopes of breathing an air fresher than the unbearable stuffiness of his own life. For two hours or so, and in a context of unreality, he goes to *believe*—in an order, an intelligibility, in splendid coincidences, necessary meetings, the possibility of harmony, sufferings that achieve something. In front of a screen or a stage, he will spend a couple of hours living in a universe where he can breathe.

Then he returns to himself and stops breathing once more. He sees only his own real life before him, and can only bow his head and flop down once more. In his own life there is no meaning; it was chance that made him marry this woman, have these children, undergo this or that grief, have that particular accident, that particular friend, that particular job, those circumstances, such a constitution—all is chance. His own life is a novel without a writer, a play with no playwright, no plot, no connecting links, no sequel, no explanation. His is a story meaning nothing, serving no purpose. He may have two hours of faith and understanding to give to others, but for himself he has only despair.

Faith is a necessity. We must have faith in other people, even if we haven't got it in God. Otherwise life would be impossible: we have to hand ourselves over, to trust. To the surgeon, for a series of humiliations, yet with complete confidence. You are made to enter hospital for ten days or so, and it is worse than a retreat: you are undressed, disturbed, made to go to bed and stay there, to live the contemplative life with a vengeance. To hamper you still further, you are put to sleep. You are opened and sliced up. In short, all kinds of things are done to you, and you stay there completely at their disposal, trusting, filial. Then you are sewn up more or less neatly. And after all that, you thank them effusively. 'That man saved my life', you will say. You believe so because he has told you so. Aren't you brave to trust him?

We believe all the time. Where is your money (if you have any)? Invested? In a bank? Is it still there? Did you go this morning to make sure? Don't you want to telephone your banker to make sure he has not absconded? Such things can happen. But no, you trust him. Suppose your money were with God? The very idea makes most people uneasy. Make God my banker? Later, perhaps; we'll see. Apparently he pays a hundred to one. Too good to be true. One cannot feel very enthusiastic. One doesn't want to offend him, but one prefers to make other arrangements.

We might as well admit that none of us really

has confidence in God. We have other, safer ways of investing our cash. They may be less remunerative, but 'a bird in the hand is worth two in the bush'. One has family commitments, responsibilities. One has no right to do anything foolish. One has no right to risk the family's property by entrusting it just to—God!

Yet we entrust our lives to the man who drives the train or bus without question. We do not ask him to show us his licence or tell us his history of accidents. We don't insist that he show us how well he drives before we enter his bus. We climb in and sit down and trust him; it is good to let someone else take charge of you—good because it is *filial*. Children always adore the driver—it is so nice to trust someone so totally, to trust a big strong man. When they get out of an aircraft, all the passengers want to shake hands with the pilot. And important travellers will shake hands with the engine-driver. He has, after all, given them one of life's greatest pleasures, by enabling them to entrust themselves to him, hand themselves over to him, to be childlike, to be what man is made to be. For we are made in the image of a Son.

Why don't we submit to this joy? Why do we always refuse to place our trust in our Father? Indeed, we positively mistrust him; it is as though when God is the driver, we want to snatch the wheel from him, or put on the brakes. When he changes direction, so that our life seems to be altering course, we utter cries of distress. When he brakes or accelerates we shout in fear or anger. Imagine a family journey with all the children telling their father what to do, shouting at every cross-roads: 'Look out, there's a coach ... See that cyclist ... You're hogging the middle of the road ...' It would be intolerable. Yet this is precisely what we do all the time with God.

Gabriel Marcel and some other contemporary philosophers have analysed the implicit faith underlying some of our most natural acts. Giving birth to a child, marrying, choosing a career, taking on any job involves an immense act of faith in something or in someone, without which we couldn't undertake anything, yet which it would be impossible to 'explain',—in someone who will keep us faithful throughout all our passing moods, who gives us a certainty of the worthwhileness of the present and the future that we cannot possibly guarantee.

To hope is to continue to love and believe, despite all the times we have been deceived, all the times we have deceived ourselves, and all the times we have deceived and betrayed others. To love is to believe ourselves capable of love despite all our infidelities, all the ups and downs of our hearts. If all this is based on nothing absolute, then all human values collapse.

Merely living means making innumerable implicit acts of faith. Unbelievers make them as much as believers, though refusing to see them as such. A book has been written on the unbelief of believers; one could also be written on the faith of unbelievers. And one may wish that the truth which the former group profess to believe may one day pass into the possession of the latter, as a reward of their faithfulness!

Sometimes we are too quick to adore; we are idolators, dedicating ourselves to a creature instead of rising from it to its Creator. But, far more often, we are too quick to condemn: we give up hope in God because creation, at the time and to the extent that we see it, is not obviously adorable. Faith knows how to wait. Guardini put it in these splendid words: 'Believing is being able to bear one's doubts.' Like Mary, faith keeps and meditates in its heart many things which it doesn't understand fully at once, but which will bear fruit in patience.

In our order of things, everything human is at the same time necessarily supernatural (caused, used, helped, filled, matured by grace). How can anyone come to a true understanding of it without being aware of this new dimension?

What gives rise to faith and feeds it is a kind of perpetual miracle, but a miracle in the moral order. A physical miracle is an event that surpasses the ordinary forces of nature. But there also exists—and indeed they are far more plentiful—moral miracles. We know more or less what we can do and what we cannot. Indeed, we are better able to judge the limits which we know by experience, than to determine what is or is not possible according to the scientific laws of the physical world. The believer, then, is the person who is aware, in himself and in others, of acts and facts which exceed man's powers, and which therefore indicate a divine intervention.

Physical miracles awe us. But the moral miracle which continually transfigures within each of us our human capabilities, so that God can love, believe and hope in us, and so that, in spite of our inadequacies, Christ in his church may be constantly present within us—surely this is more overwhelming still. What can be the explanation for thousands and thousands of noble, generous, and clear-headed people praying, going to mass, and receiving communion, unless it be that they have found strength and support from doing so, have found an answer to their prayer, a reality beneath the appearances? What sustains and justifies a religious life is not the arguments of apologetics, but the certainty of being in contact with a presence that nourishes them. In prayer, for instance, man feels himself so deeply, sometimes even so painfully, stirred and transformed that he is forced to admit that only God could act so profoundly upon him. We can all try to cooperate with that transforming power, feeling gradually how the dispositions with which we began change under the influence of prayer. We can sense our soul becoming gradually modelled upon another. We can become stripped of our human ambitions, cleansed of self-interest, detached from our paltry interests, and miraculously strengthened to accept what would before have seemed impossible.

All those who have once had such an experience—have felt themselves extraordinarily touched, raised up, enlarged by this life-giving force of prayer, this as it were bathing of the soul in the sun of supernatural life—are unmoved by being asked how they would answer this or that objection, how solve this or that difficulty. Before one has experienced the reality, a thousand proofs do not add up to certainty. Afterwards, ten thousand difficulties, as Newman said, do not make one doubt.

We have all, at some time in our lives, perceived God in some such way, whether through the joy we feel when we let ourselves be thus guided by a light we have glimpsed, or the sorrow when we have rejected it. After some sacrifice, or some period of exceptional generosity, we see with astonishment what we have been doing, and can hardly recognise ourself in it. We cannot understand how we can have been so good, or so generous, or how being so can have come so easily to us. We feel that somehow we have been lifted out of ourselves, that there was someone else within us, bearing our burden.

Man today has a dangerous, but direct, method of judging truth: he refers to man, to the kind of man he will become if he lives by it. And the christian can prove the truth of what he believes by experiencing the Christ he is becoming through prayer and the life of charity. Easy to see then, why faith can so easily be lost, and how one must set about finding it again. A life of prayer and generosity makes the presence and influence of him in whom we believe more and more evident to us. Lukewarmness, on the other hand, slackness in prayer, selfishness—all these weaken or kill in us that religious life which seems so unreal when we no longer possess it.

How apt here are Christ's words:

To every one who has will more be given; but from him who has not, even what he has will be taken away. [Mt 25:29.]

Fervent christians see a thousand indications of God's inspiration and providence—the joy one gets from a good action, the strength one gains from prayer, the shame one feels at having disregarded a good impulse, the times when circumstances should combine to overwhelm us totally but mercifully turn out to help us. Everything that can only be fully explained supernaturally— every such thing is a sign, a miracle for those who, having experienced God, recognise him unhesitatingly in his smallest manifestation—just as it is said that a man can recognise his wife from a single hair.

The non-fervent call for miracles that will bring the experience of God into the only order that interests them—the material. But God is sparing with those, for he fears to make their interest in it greater still. 'You seek me,' said our Lord, after the feeding of the five thousand, 'not because you saw signs, but because you ate your fill of the loaves' (Jn 6:26). A miracle is a translation into the physical order of God's constant interventions in the moral order. The insensitive and uncultivated cannot, so to say, read the divine text without such a translation into their own language; to understand and follow the original text requires an attentive and sensitive reader.

The believer is one who, like Mary, 'keeps' all

the events of his life, even—and perhaps especially —the painful and the incomprehensible ones, and ponders them in his heart, trying to discern God's mark upon them, to receive them as God's invitation. The believer is one who has the reverence to respect the element of mystery in everything that happens to him, who gives way neither to wild enthusiasm nor to wild despair. He doesn't cry, 'I understand completely', or moan, 'I don't understand at all'. He remembers Mary and Joseph who 'did not understand the saying which he spoke to them' (Lk 2 : 50), and doesn't expect to understand everything immediately, but rather to be outstripped, disturbed, kept on the move. But never despairing. Never his whole heart given to joy, which is childish; never so sad that there is room for no other feeling, which is blasphemy. God is God.

We must always be ready to say, 'It may be better so. This is surely not what it seems—this injustice, this indifference, this cruelty, this absurdity. This wasted suffering. This game. God doesn't make toys of us—not of any of us. He will explain it to me one day'. The third day he rose again from the dead. But even then there was another wait until Pentecost before things were really made clear. It is up to us to remain open, ready, to trust God, to look forward to that understanding of the things of God which is given to the humble, to the subjects of the beatitudes.

3
In God, the Father almighty, Creator of heaven and earth

To say that God is Creator is another way of saying that he is Father; had he not been Father, he would not have been Creator. It was being Father that made him want to create. Because he was infinitely pleased in his Son, he wanted sons, and it was in the image of his Son that he made the world. His creation was an overflowing of love and delight.

The doctrine books tell us that 'God created the world for his glory'. But 'his glory' is to show how much he loves; it is his joy in having a Son, and having sons and daughters. What kind of father would have children 'for his glory', for himself? If such a dreadful thing happened, wouldn't it be a contradiction? It certainly doesn't happen with God. God does not absorb others, but pours himself out upon them; he is giving and love. He who loves creates by the very fact of loving, and with all the freedom and generosity of love. By loving one produces more love all round one, 'creating' an overflow of love, and therefore of life. Living means loving: 'We know that we have passed from death to life, *because we love* the brethren (1 Jn 3:14). To love is to call to life. Those who love us awaken in us a response of love, an upsurge of life; in the same way, it is by his paternal love that God creates us.

God is Father, he is love, he is almighty: God is Creator. Anyone who doesn't believe that his existence is at every moment the effect of God's love turned upon him is an atheist. For even though he may believe in a God, it is not the God of the creed. The God of the creed is a God who loves.

Really to see God in this light calls for hours of contemplation and prayer. One must be 'exposed' to God for some time to stop being an atheist, to be touched by the radiance of the Father, and awakened to faith, and to emulation. Though the Father is among us as bread to eat ('My food is to do the will of him who sent me', Jn 4:34), though he is a force that can give strength to us, though he is a paternity capable of arousing in us the love of giving, we need long contemplation before we can be penetrated by him. That is the purpose of our vigils, of hours spent before the blessed sacrament. Only thus can we fulfil our Lord's words:

> I . . . accomplished the work which thou gavest me to do; . . . I have manifested thy name to the men whom thou gavest me out of the world; . . . they have believed that thou didst send me. [Jn 17:4, 6, 8.]

If we don't believe, don't feel in us that joy and gratitude towards the Father who is constantly creating us by loving us, and loving us as he creates us; if God's will in causing *me* to exist at this moment doesn't seem to me good—it is because I have not tried hard enough to see him as he is, nor thought enough about him, nor prayed enough. I haven't been nourished by him, nor exposed myself properly to his beneficent light.

> We all, with unveiled face, beholding the glory of the Lord, are being changed into his likeness from one degree of glory to another; for this comes from the Lord who is the Spirit. [2 Cor 3:18.]

'Send forth thy Spirit, and they shall be created' —we shall suddenly find ourselves able to hope, to believe, to love in our turn. We shall rediscover ourselves—as fathers, mothers, created, creating. God has manifested his paternal power throughout nature. All creation is in some sense God-become-visible. Nature in its deepest reality is in a state of happy contemplation, reflecting God, offering thanks, giving back, announcing what it has received, hymning that which it resembles. Where we invoke, nature evokes him in whose image it has been created.

The Father's generosity is imprinted on nature. That is why contemplating it brings us close to him. What we strive uneasily to glimpse, nature reflects in joy. That is why the saints have sometimes felt such an extraordinary closeness to 'my sister water, my brother the sun, my brother fire', and so on—those silent, modest adorers, whose 'lifetime' is spent contemplating the same face as they do.

The covenant with Noah is the confirmation, the renewal of this harmony. The rainbow was a sign of God's covenant with the whole world. All men are invited to enter that harmony: there is a kind of knowledge of God, a kind of invitation to enter into alliance with him through the intermediary of all that is beautiful, good, and well ordered in the world.

What can be known about God is plain to them, because God has shown it to them. Ever since the creation of the world his invisible nature . . . has been clearly perceived in the things that have been made. [Rom 1:19f.]

The God who made the world and everything in it, being Lord of heaven and earth, does not live in shrines made by man, nor is he served by human hands, as though he needed anything, since he himself gives to all men life and breath and everything. And he made from one every nation of men to live on all the face of the earth, having determined allotted periods [the reference is to the covenant with Noah— the promise that there would be no more floods and that there would be order in the world, with regular seasons] . . . that they should seek God, in the hope that they might feel after him and find him. Yet he is not far from each one of us, for 'In him we live and move and have our being'. [Acts 17:24–8.]

This groping discovery of a divine principle, this unformulated respect for a sovereign authority governing the seasons and their order, this obscure sense of paternal goodness inscribed in the laws of nature, this is the covenant with God as far as most pagans apprehend it. For pagans are 'backward'. They are (religiously) the same age as Noah. They are several covenants behind us—Abraham, Moses, Christ. They have the rainbow where we have the eucharist. We need not smile over their simplicity by comparison with us, nor be proud of our superiority; we have done nothing to deserve it. We have been given it. And we have kept it to ourselves! We are in fact gravely guilty for not yet having succeeded in sharing it with all mankind. They will not go to hell without us, but we are in serious danger of going there without them. We are responsible for them; we are the developed people, the educators. And we do not educate. We are the saviours, and we save no one. It may well be easier to be saved in Kamchatka than in the Vatican. If the pagans are faithful to their covenant, venerating what can be seen of God in nature and respecting the moral law inscribed in their hearts (Rom 2:15), then they are doing all that God requires of them. They are assured of the return of the seasons, they assent to the movement of the tides, they have a kind of confidence in life.

In the covenant of Noah, one's harmony with God depends on one's harmony with nature. But we, who have received the whole of revelation, who have been invited to such a tremendous covenant with God—what about us?

> I have given them the words which thou gavest me . . . That they may be one even as we are one, I in them and thou in me, . . . so that the world may know that thou . . . hast loved them even as thou has loved me. [Jn 17:8, 22f.] As thou didst send me into the world, so I have sent them into the world. [Jn 17:18.]

But have we gone? Have we done Christ's will? Are we faithful? Do we long for that glory, assent to that word? Are we raised up by that love? Nature was our younger sister, but it has remained so much more faithful an image of what it was called to signify that it may well have grown beyond us—more faithful, more like our Father. Man has indeed sometimes distorted nature, with atomic explosions and gas chambers—he has done all he can to disfigure it until it looks like himself. (This may well account for the horror of certain completely rational creations of man—certain factories, pieces of music, pictures, railway stations.) Man has, as it were, created in nature an image of his own revolt.

If, then, nature is good, if creation is the faithful image of an almighty Father, how comes it that there is so much evil in the world? All human philosophies come finally to this question. But the answer is not a philosophical one. The answer is in the creed. God—Father, almighty— is Creator: *of heaven and earth.* The Nicene creed specifies further: and *of all things, visible and in-*

visible. This is a formal protest against any dualist solution to the problem of evil—and dualism of this kind remains a tendency with us all. St Augustine himself was attracted to manicheism for a very long time, and the church has had to work hard to free christian thought of all traces of it.

Manicheism and all other dualist systems declare that there are two principles, one good, one evil. The good one has created spirit—angels, our souls, all that belongs to the 'spiritual' life. The evil one has created the world, the 'flesh', bodies. Therefore: all that is earthly is evil, all that is spiritual is good. The only way to redemption is to become detached from the body, this 'worthless trash', and become purely a soul, a beautiful soul —disengaged and detached. The church has solemnly condemned this idea. We are not required to become beautiful souls. The Lord is the creator of men—that is of bodily beings animated by life-giving spirits. And to redeem them, far from suggesting that they try to escape from their bodies, he himself became incarnate. To identify christianity with any kind of dualism is a scandal. A christian cannot be a dualist or an idealist; he that has such an exaggerated wish to save his soul shall lose it. Christ became incarnate. He took flesh—the word was made flesh and dwelt amongst us—that by doing so he might redeem the world. Not from a distance, but from close by; not invisibly alone, but visibly. And he has left us his body—to eat! Daily.

The church believes that there is only one

Creator, that all things were created by God, and that in everything that exists there is an indelible mark of his paternal goodness. To explain the origin of evil by a duality of creation is false and dangerous: false, because under the pretext of making God thus innocent of evil it diminishes him by taking half of his creation from him; and dangerous, because it counsels man to flight as the means of redemption. It prescribes escape, withdrawal from the world, renunciation of the things of earth. But God, on the contrary, loves the world. He has not rejected the flesh he created. He has so loved the world as to give his only-begotten Son (cf. Jn 3:16). To take refuge in 'spiritual' attitudes is to move in precisely the opposite direction to God. God saves *in* the incarnation.

To the church, the origin of evil does not lie in the flesh. The sin of Adam was a sin not of the flesh but of the spirit. As far as one can observe, the flesh of its nature is healthier than the spirit. There are no drunkards, for instance, among the animals, but only among men. To drink only when you are thirsty—that is to be like the animals. We do not drug ourselves with alcohol because we have a taste for drink, but because we have a distaste for life. It is a sin of the spirit. Lust and debauchery originate, not in sexuality, but in infidelity, in a (spiritual) desire for something new, for a change, for variety; it is an attempt to satisfy our need for the infinite with a variety of the indefinite; it betrays a kind of despair. A man who fails to preserve any satisfactory emotional relationships with others will try to escape from his miserable loneliness by seeking this way and that, by multiplying contacts in which all he is doing is colliding with the walls of his own prison. Blondel puts it well: 'The spirit commands the body and is obeyed; the spirit commands itself and is resisted.'

The sins of the flesh are the least serious. The church, like all of us, seems sometimes to believe the opposite. And it is this which in fact leads most people to drift away from God and from religious practice. But the church's true doctrine is quite definite in placing the 'mortal' principle of sin in the spirit. The worst sin is not telling God that one 'can't' obey all his commandments; it is trying to do without him altogether, in pride or in despair.

To scorn the body, to decry the pleasures God offers us in the world of the senses, is to cast aside his work and reject what he has made. 'God saw that it was good' is the refrain that expresses the whole meaning of Genesis. The Genesis creation story is a poem, joyfully enumerating all that was created, and after each verse the refrain comes as a delighted approbation, a confirmation that the flesh, the body, the world, all things visible, are good. Plants, light, water—all are glorious. Yet, incredibly, we do not feel too sure. We mistrust; we criticise; and when we chance to taste something good, when we are for once of God's opinion, in agreement with God, we suddenly feel that we have committed a sin. Though we may find God's gifts delightful, we think at once that they must be traps.

The explanation given in Genesis—and propounded by christianity—of the origin of the world and the destiny of man, is in fact the only one which does *not* set up an opposition between the material and the spiritual, but on the contrary incarnates the one in the other, so that the flesh has a spiritual significance—the body being the sign, the expression, the form, of the spirit with which it always remains linked. In the biblical and christian explanation of the world, the spirit is not veiled by matter, but expressed through it. Whatever is not thus expressed, what is in no way 'figured' or 'realised', must simply fade and die, or vanish into smoke (very superior smoke, of course!). We look forward with longing, not to a 'kingdom of souls', but to the resurrection of the body. That is to be our future. We shall enter eternity, not as so many holy wraiths, but as men, body and soul.

The world is God-made-visible, God appearing in matter. God, the Light, is reflected, and manifested in a thousand images which refract him, a thousand aspects of him taking shape—'being made flesh'—in the world and in us. God is communicable, and it is through these things he has made that he communicates himself. Creation is always what he wills; when it was damaged he repaired it so that it might remain a worthy image of him. The redemption is just as original as sin.

But if all that God has created is good, if the origin of evil is not God, nor the flesh, nor the body, nor matter, how are we to explain the existence of evil in the world? Genesis tells us at once: it is sin. A blundering wish for independence, a refusal to depend on anyone; a failure to recognise the joy of being poor. Adam made unhappiness for himself by rejecting the first beatitude. His rejection was an utter mistake. Original sin was a muddle, in which Adam thought independence meant the same thing as liberty. He was free—not floating, indeterminate, autonomous and alone, but capable of perfect love, capable of joyfully depending on someone else (which is what love means). And he wanted to stop depending, to 'know' on his own account, to refuse the obedience God requires.

God, who is all gift, wants his sons to be like him. So much does he want to share his own life with us, so much does he want us to taste his own joy, that he wants to give us the power to give. But from the moment of willing that, God accepted in a certain sense a curtailment of his own power. Can God need men? God willed to need them; he willed man to be able to resist him, willed him to be free, to be in his turn a creator. God is so totally a creator that he wanted his creation to be creative; he wanted man to be able to originate, for that is what freedom means—originating something, doing the unforeseen. When we say that God made man free, that means genuinely free. It was not just that man looked free, that he acted as though he were free. It was that there was something in man's will which could elude God unless man chose to give it to him.

Does this mean God is not omnipotent? No. He could have done without us, but in the plan of creation and then of redemption that he chose, he created us able to respond to him or to refuse, to collaborate with him or not. He wanted us to be saviours, responsible for one another; he willed there to be intercessions, sacraments, means of salvation, a communion of saints; he willed that men should act upon one another, that there should be transformation of man by other men. That is why we must pray for one another.

Man, who can resist God, can also give himself freely to him. This trust—this joyful, original, willed, free, and fervent submission—is the only response God was interested in getting from man. To get it, he had to run the risk he ran. One may think that since that risk is for man a mortal risk, he should in his goodness have avoided it. But his goodness is such, the power of his love is such, that he could at once face that risk and over-come it.

God knew his own fatherhood so well as to be certain that by the force of his paternal love not all men would resist him. He believed that he would find in every generation the amount of hope and of love necessary for the salvation of the rest—that there would always be people who would be willing to become saviours, redeemers. He dared to have such hope for us because his paternal power was great enough to be able always to raise up among us fathers and mothers —men and women who would let themselves be so filled with him as to be able to bear the burden of all the rest, and finally to achieve the happy fulfilment of his will on earth as in heaven. God willed that there should be a kind of emulation, a rivalry in creativity, between him and man. But the power and the persistence of his love assured him of winning the contest, and of repairing any harm that might come of it by his own inventiveness and suffering.

Whatever new ways we may think up of betraying him and escaping him, whatever our next sin may be, God knows that we shall barely have finished committing it before his longing to call us back and have us return to him will lead him to think of a new way to make himself loved by us; he will light on a new and unexpected appeal that will touch us and draw us back to him however far we have fled. For the God of the philosophers, of course, who is immobile, immovable, invulnerable, insensible, and irrevocable, the world was ruled out like music paper, with sin foreseen, and the incarnation ready as the automatic answer to it. And so it has all taken place, each playing his hand in turn. We are allowed to join in to make life a bit more exciting—but the excitement wears thin after a while, especially if we must believe it to be only play-acting which will make no difference to the outcome. If that is the case, why doesn't God give up the pretence, and directly assign everyone to his appointed place in heaven, hell, or purgatory, without further ado? But the gospel never gives us this sense of detachment which one would feel in the case of a foregone conclusion. Certainly there is a plan, an unfolding, a will, an hour for Christ to confront and achieve, but it all takes place in complete freedom; it all signifies a supreme effort on God's part to keep us, to call us back, to beg us to respond to him.

Adam abused his freedom, but it was *felix culpa*, for the Word was made flesh and dwelt amongst us. Eve brought about the fall, but God gave us Mary, with the annunciation and all its freshness, its joy, its acceptance. Only after his sin did David become able to sing really well to the Lord. His wickedness was followed by a new revelation and a new series of promises. Afterwards his love was greater: his repentance, so magnificent, so simple, so immediate, laid him open to receive a new gift. God at once promised him forgiveness: 'The Lord has put away your sin' (2 Sam 12:13), Nathan told him. The response was ready. God is strong enough and Father enough to be ready even for our sins.

4
And in Jesus Christ, his only Son, our Lord

In the longer creed we sing at Mass, we say: 'In one Lord Jesus Christ, the only-begotten Son of God, born of the Father before time began. God from God, Light from Light, true God from true God; begotten, not made, one in substance with the Father; and through him all things were made. For us men and for our salvation he came down from heaven, ... and was made man'.

What idea have we formed of God? How do we address him? What is our picture of him? What representation of him do we prefer to pray before? (This gives a strong indication of the nature of our religion and our relationship with heaven.) How do we present God to our children, our friends, and everyone else who could learn more about him from us?

We cannot decide for ourselves how to incarnate the idea of God, for God has made the decision himself. We can only 'picture' his existence in one way, because the picture already exists. This fact is of capital importance. Yet we all tend, with incredible lightheartedness, to cast it aside, and daily create our own picture of God—avenging, imperturbable, distant. We constantly deck God out in the attributes that we—sinful, ambitious, and selfish—consider suitable to the divinity. God, said Voltaire, has created man in his image and likeness, and man has returned the compliment.

Because God wants us to understand him, he has told us that he is Father, that he is Son, and that their Spirit is love. He has revealed to us that in him there are three who share all things ('All that is thine is mine'), and that it is to that communion of life that he wants to join us. We know, now, that to be as God wills us to be—in his likeness—means to be in a group who love one another and love those outside. God is love working to save those who do not yet love. 'God so loved the world that he gave his only Son' (Jn 3: 16). How can we still think of God as solitary, apart, immovable, invulnerable? All too many christians set out to picture God by discounting the best in themselves—their capacity for love and self-denial.

God is the being who has to be several to be himself. Are we like him? If we feel that we are more 'ourselves' when we are alone, serene, aloof, withdrawn from the world, completely self-possessed in fact, it means that we are truly excommunicated, cut off from the communion that reflects the community of God—cut off from the only state that is, in sober truth, heavenly. It means that we prefer what is of hell: solitude, autonomy, satanic in-dependence.

What we discover from community, from team-work, from group life, is that the joy of co-operation develops all our powers for good. We gradually find that the presence of those around us who love us makes us more worthwhile people; that we are better, work better, become more daring and more confident, thanks to other people who lean on us and accept to receive without fuss whatever we have to give them. It is the same with marriage. A real wife, if her husband is not there, feels—or should feel—paralysed, lost, incapable of making decisions which she would make with no difficulty were he there. She doesn't know what she thinks until he has said what he thinks (then, of course, she knows very well, and her opinion seldom coincides with his!). And a real husband, without his wife, without that loving presence who collaborates in all he does and simply by being there shows him whether he has done right or wrong—without her, he is unsure of himself, dis-couraged, helpless. He finds life hardly worth the trouble of living, and slips into the rough-and-ready existence of a neglected bachelor.

'Not in the singularity of one person', says the preface of the Trinity: there is no God, there is no man, there is no love in the isolation or selfishness of a single person. God does not live withdrawn in an ivory tower; he exists in unceasing communica-tion, and invites us to do the same thing. If you want to know whether you are really a christian, ask yourself what you would think if you were suddenly told: the blessed Trinity is not a dogma. We must still believe that there is only one God, but we need no longer believe that there are three persons. I think many people would say, 'Well, it will be a lot easier to explain God to the children'; or, 'One less difficulty for unbelievers to be asked to swallow'. How many of us respond to the Trinity simply as a difficult combination of algebra and theology?

'You need no longer believe that God is love'; would that produce consternation? How much joy has that belief given me? Am I one of those who would feel quite happy as long as they are told that God remains just. 'That's all right, then! He will still recognise my merits as before.'

The Trinity (the dogma of the Trinity) ought rather to be the answer to all our discouragements and troubles. 'They love one another. We must therefore also love one another. And in the end we will if we really work at it.' The commandment to love one another cannot be separated from the revelation of the Trinity. They are the same thing. We must be charity because God is Trinity. There is no place in christianity for happiness in solitude. The Holy Spirit helps us not to do without other people (that job is done by the devil) but to be unable to do without them. 'Not in the singularity of one person . . .' His consolation will consist in making us better able to love those who have wounded us—not to be able, with his help, to forget them.

God is wholly Father. We can be something of a father, something of a worker, something of a citizen, something of a philanthrope, something of an apostle, something of a husband or wife, partly responsible for this or that; God is totally Father. And he has a Son who resembles him totally:

I glorified thee on earth . . . ; and now, Father, glorify thou me . . . The world has not known thee, but I have known thee. [Jn 17:4f, 25.]

The Son's whole life is praise, revealing the Father. 'These things I speak in the world, that they may have my joy fulfilled in themselves' (Jn 17:13): his joy is to know the Father. Our joy, when we hear the gospel, should be to learn from it to know the Father; the gospel is, after all, his revelation.

The 'good news' is that sins are forgiven. God is a Father who forgives. All the gospel is summed up in the parable of the prodigal son, for the whole history of salvation is there: all man's wickedness, original sin ('give me the share of property that falls to me', Lk 15:12), all the defenceless, solicitous goodness of God—'While he was yet at a distance, his father saw him and had compassion, and ran to him and embraced him and kissed him' (Lk 15:20). That is, of course, God, our Father.

The Son died to show us—to unveil (re-veal)—the Father in this, his true, light. The Son died to demonstrate his Father's goodness. Yet we still seem sometimes almost to believe that he came to protect us from his Father's anger. We aren't forbidden to sing that terrible passiontide hymn, *Man of sorrows, wrapt in grief*; year after year

there are those who think to please God by singing, with a sob in their voices, that

> Thou for us the path hast trod
> Of the dreadul wrath of God;
> Thou the cup of fire hast drained . . .

'Have I been with you so long, and yet you do not
know me . . .?' (Jn 14:9). You have understood
nothing! 'He who has seen me has seen the
Father.' Whether in the crib, or on the cross, it is
equally true; it was to tell us that he came to die
on earth.

'Why didn't the Father himself come?' some
will object. He did something better still: he gave
us the best thing he had. 'God so loved the world
that he gave his only Son' (Jn 3:16). Which would
we find harder to do—die ourselves, or watch a
child of ours die? We have but to ask the question to see at once that if Calvary was worse for
one or the other, it was worse for the Father. 'God
so loved the world that he gave his only Son'—
that he was ready to sacrifice his own Son. It is
good to ponder *that* crucifixion, too, when we
make the 'way of the cross'. *Never* must we think
of the Son without the Father: 'all mine are thine,
and thine are mine' (Jn 17:10).

We shall never be closer to the Son than when
we stop thinking of him in isolation, and, 'following his divine initiative, we make bold to say,
"Our Father . . ." '. With him. In him. Through
him. In his last prayer, Christ prayed 'that the
world may know that thou hast sent me and hast
loved them even as thou hast loved me' (Jn 17:

54

23). Yet many christians still don't truly know or believe that the Son is the Father's love made visible.

What was our Lord thinking about as he walked along the roads of Galilee, so often alone (on occasions such as that when the disciples fell behind him to carry on their favourite dispute as to who among them should be greatest, Mk 9: 32f.)? What were his thoughts in times of repose, during the journeys by boat that he liked making with his disciples after a day's exhausting preaching? What occupied his mind among the hills where he liked to withdraw alone, without even the disciples? The answer, we may think, is easy: he was thinking of men, of sinners and their salvation, and what he had to do to effect that salvation. But, surprising as it may seem to us, it wasn't with us that Jesus was concerned. The constant object of his meditation, the natural orientation of his heart and mind and soul, the food that constantly nourished him, was his Father.

Remember his meeting with the Samaritan woman. He sat, weary, beside the well—the disciples went to the village, but he stayed. He was waiting for the Samaritan woman and that wonderful conversation he was to have with her (Jn 4). And it was in this sinful woman that he found someone who would listen to him and understand the thing nearest his heart—he had found someone to whom he could speak of his Father, and for that reason he was refreshed, satisfied, fed. When the disciples returned and settled down cheerfully to eat, they suddenly realised that he wasn't with them; distressed, as one is when one is enjoying food in front of someone who is thinking of other things, they said, 'Rabbi eat' (Jn 4:31). 'But he said to them, "I have food to eat of which you do not know"' (v. 32). With their usual literal-mindedness they misunderstood him, and asked one another who could have given him food, but he replied: 'My food is to do the will of him who sent me' (v. 34). This had actually satisfied his hunger! And when he was in the desert, we are told, 'he ate nothing in those days; and when they were ended, he was hungry' (Lk 4:2). As long as he was praying, he was nourished—he missed nothing.

All Christ's interior life was a life of reverent and affectionate intimacy with his Father. Before being Mary's son and our brother, he is the Father's Son. From babyhood he rejoiced in his poverty because it exposed him to the Father, it placed him totally in his Father's hands—for it is good to expose oneself wholly and completely to the Father's will. He was a Son who, with unparalleled daring, wanted to be totally 'Son', in order that he might reveal the extent of the Father's fatherhood.

It was this overpowering filial urge that kept him in the temple when he was twelve. He went there with the yearly pilgrims, in that special atmosphere of merriment that goes with faith and festivals. He went into a place where, for the first time in his life, he felt at home and happy. At last he had found a place in the world where everything was worship, reverence, and thanksgiving, just as he was himself. So he remained there in wonderment; he felt peaceful, sustained, balanced, at home. And when they came to look for him, his reply was not flippant, but simply surprised: You went away? You were able to leave this house where everything speaks of my Father, where one feels at home with him? Why did you seek me? Could you think I would be anywhere but with my Father?

Some of the loveliest and most moving passages in the gospel are those in which Christ speaks to us of his Father. God is a Father whose goodness is universal, making his sun to shine on the just and the unjust, and his rain to rain upon them all. He is a watchful and loving Father, whose eyes are always upon us, who sees the alms we give in secret, the humble prayer we say alone, who knows our needs better than we do. He gives to those who ask, opens to those who knock; he feeds the birds of the air and clothes the lilies of the field. He doesn't lose sight of even a single sparrow, and has numbered the very hairs of our heads. He is the careful husbandman who puts up patiently with the cockle for fear of damaging the wheat. He is the lord of the vineyard who rises early to hire workers, and then is so anxious for the welfare of others that he goes again at the third, the sixth, the ninth, the eleventh hours, so that no one shall be unemployed, disappointed, left out.

Our Lord works hard to make us cease to fear this great and majestic God. He likens him to a humble housewife who has lost a coin, and lights the lamp, sweeps the house, searching high and low—and then shares with all her neighbours the joy of having at last found it. The Father, whom we imagine as a severe critic of everything we do, an inflexible judge of our sins, is a father so kind and even weak that he lets his son go off with his inheritance—but goes every day to watch for his return, and when he sees him in the distance, runs to meet him, and embrace him. And who then apologises humbly to his enraged elder son:

> Son, you are always with me, and all that is mine is yours. It was fitting to make merry and be glad, for this your brother was dead, and is alive; he was lost, and is found. [Lk 15:31f.]

The Father can never refuse to answer prayer, and Christ even goes so far as to compare him with an unjust judge who gives way to requests not because he is just, but because he cannot be bothered to go on rejecting them. We need only wonder whether we are bold enough, confident enough, in playing upon God's weakness towards us!

'[Father,] I have accomplished the work which thou gavest me to do ... I have manifested thy name to men ...' (Jn 17:4, 6). To have manifested his *name* means to have given us a permanent advantage over *him*. A name for the ancients meant something quite different from what it means to us. To call something by its name was a sign, a means of power. Adam could name the animals because God had given man authority over creation. In antiquity, it was a crime to reveal to foreigners the names of one's country's gods; for, if they were properly addressed, they would obey outsiders as well as their own people. Once the name was revealed, the covenant was broken.

By inviting us to say, 'Father', Christ was sharing with us his greatest wealth, that 'power' which was given to him in heaven and on earth, the power of a child over its parents—all the privileges of a Son. 'That the world may know that thou ... hast loved them even as thou hast loved me' (Jn 17:23). Christ's teaching, the work he had been given to do, was just that: Call him 'Father', be no longer afraid, say 'Our Father'. A true father and a true mother have no defences against their children. Christ could do nothing greater for us than giving us his Father. We are the true Israel, for we have 'striven with God' (Gen 32:28)—if, that is, we have learnt to say, if we dare to say and mean, 'Father'.

5
And was made man

'Blessed is he who takes no offence at me' (Mt 11:6). Men have always been scandalised by God, by his silence or his word, by his intervening or failing to intervene, by his punishments or his forgiveness. But never have they been more scandalised than by his incarnation. The incarnation is the love of God made visible. It isn't surprising, then, that mankind haven't yet ceased —indeed, have barely begun—to measure all its dimensions, its length and breadth, its height and depth. Though twenty centuries prepared for it, and it has been proclaimed for twenty more, it remains the most difficult of all dogmas to take in —the target of all heresies, the crux of all doctrines—, for it admits neither of escape into pure spirituality, nor of refuge in pure materialism, but calls for a perpetual confrontation of man in his reality with the true God—a confrontation which must be harmonised in every individual's religious life.

60

Europe, we are told by a Hindu sage, has not yet understood half of Christ's message. It has understood that Christ and God are one. But it has yet to discover the other half—that Christ and man are one: that man, everyman, the least of men, is Christ's.

The incarnation is a scandal to the Jews. It abases the Most High, defiling what is Holy in the uncleanness of birth, of blood, and of death. 'A hanged man is accursed by God' (Deut 21:23). He whom a man cannot see and live, who allows no graven image, is suddenly made visible, and is then disfigured. Yet Hebrew thought had long been preparing for this mystery: man made in God's likeness, matter created by his word, declared good, and fitted to be a symbol of spirit. Wine, water, bread, rocks, oil, indeed all creation, had always had a sacramental sense for the Israelites. And the word was the very means God used to reveal himself. That is why the word was made flesh—but 'his own people received him not' (Jn 1:11).

The incarnation is folly to the Greeks. It puts what is eternal into time, what is spirit into matter, what is one into what is many, the universal into the particular. It follows precisely the opposite path to the Greek idealism that looks for salvation in ceasing to be incarnate.

But still more it is something too large and too disconcerting for us all—christians of today and of the past. All the major heresies indicate our resistance to this dizzy ideal, this incongruous and upsetting bringing together of man and God in a real union. Ebionites, manicheans, arians, nestorians, moslems have denied it. Docetists declared it to be only an appearance. Monophysites and monothelites absorb the humanity into the divinity. Every possible way out of the scandal has been tried. And all these heresies still live. We of the twentieth century are as permeated by them as men of an earlier age.

There is the modern appolinarianism so common among ill-instructed christians of believing Jesus appeared in a body with no human soul, and taking the word *flesh* to mean no more than *meat*. In biblical language, however, *flesh* means the whole human reality with all its pitiful weakness, but also with its possibility of being elevated by the Spirit of God. In this sense, the soul is the most 'carnal' part of man, for it is the soul that commits the greatest 'carnal' sin of all, pride.

There is also the docetism of the theologian who, in the charming simile of a friend of mine, represents Christ as someone on a motorised bicycle pretending that it is an ordinary push-bike to encourage the other cyclists. He makes a pretence of pushing hard on the pedals, he gives an occasional sigh to suggest fatigue, he mops his face because others are sweating. Of these is the pious exegete who said that Jesus prayed 'to give us a good example'; or this comment of Bossuet on the text of Lk 2:52 ('Jesus increased in wisdom and in stature'): 'Jesus possessed all perfection from the first, but only let it appear gradually, so that he would seem like a real child.' There is the monophysitism of those who think

Jesus was once a man, but is now only—and for ever—God. There is, above all, the nestorianism (in practice) of the innumerable christians who exclude Christ from the world. They put him in heaven, and burn incense to him and get him out of the way, and then they can make fraternal charity at the most a commandment, a 'test' of love for God, a trial, an opportunity for merit, a springboard to heaven. For there is a docetist doctrine of charity as well as of the incarnation: Christ looked upon the good done to the least of his little ones 'as if' it were done to him.

The Word became flesh. [Jn 1 : 14.]
    In him all the fullness of God was pleased to dwell. [Col 1 : 19.]

If you want to feel the initial shock, the primitive (and necessary) scandal of these phrases—by now too familiar to affect us much—, try saying, 'God became woman', or, 'God is my neighbour'. Mary Magdalen took him for a gardener. The disciples on the road to Emmaus walked for miles with him without even recognising him, so common-place was he! Yet all of revelation is the epic of the progressive incarnation of God communicating himself to us in ways suited to us—ways which we must therefore believe to be also suitable to him, human and material ways. 'No man has ever seen God' (1 Jn 4 : 12; cf. Jn 1 : 18), nor ever can, for he 'dwells in unapproachable light' (1 Tim 6 : 16). It's no use trying to capture him by ascetic feats, or to lay hold of him by any trick of contemplative experience. God is an 'unknown

God' to the wise and the proud. 'The Lord has said that he would dwell in thick darkness' (2 Chron 6:1; cf. 1 Kings 8:12), at least as far as those who want to take possession of him are concerned. But he reveals himself freely to the poor and humble, and does so at their level— the human level—, and by simple means, using material forms.

Our first reaction to this is one of surprise. We are more accustomed to the idea that God requires faith, submission, and incomprehension. Yet it is true to say that God is light, revelation, epiphany. What makes the christian religion different from all others is that it is a religion of incarnation, a sacramental religion in which God reveals himself and is always revealed to our senses.

In the bible the invisible is truly expressed in the visible (cf. Rom 1:20), the divine in the human, the thing signified in the sign, the grace in the sacrament. Beginning with man's creation in God's image, this intended proportion, this possibility of communication between him and us was always signified. 'When God formed Adam's body', said the fathers, 'he thought of Christ who would one day become man.' Man was created receptive to God. In paradise, God came to converse familiarly with Adam in the cool of the evening. God made himself understood; he communicated with Adam in a human way; he confided in Adam. Adam entered God's confidence; and when someone talks to us freely about himself, we say he *delivers* himself to us.

Thus the passion, that revelation of God's love in all its boldness and vulnerability, began in the garden of Eden. Adam rejected that revelation, and entered darkness. Sin is the situation in which he is no longer known, the abnormal condition in which he is no longer attainable by our senses. The darkness did not take possession of God; rather it rejected him altogether.

But God didn't stop there. He never ceased to express himself, to reveal himself, drawing back the veil of darkness that has fallen between himself and us. He called Abraham, and Abraham heard him. Abraham had the same joy St John was later to have, of hearing him with his ears and seeing him with his eyes; he welcomed him into his tent, and had something of the meaning of God's paternity confided to him through his own experience of the most incredible birth and the most agonising sacrifice. When God commanded Moses to lead his people to the desert, Moses replied: 'If thy presence will not go with me, do not carry us up from here' (Ex 33:15). Without the 'real presence', without their sacrament, they would never have had the courage to cross the desert. They needed that surety, that divine sign in their midst, just as we need the eucharist: if thy body will not go with us, send us not out into the desert!

The veil was raised higher and higher until Jesus' coming, and then it was rent from top to bottom. God became man. To see Jesus was—is—to see the Father: God has become fully human. Henceforth it is Christ's humanity that even the most ethereal mystic must contemplate, and what marks him out is that he makes a fuller use of all the signs to attain to the reality they signify. We must see him not as lost in ecstasy, but as working (for even the recitation of the office is work: *opus dei*) to find out the *meaning* of what he is doing. When he reads scripture he is listening to the word through its words. To be a contemplative is not to do nothing, but to see a lot; not to do less work than others, but to see more clearly; to be, not naïve, but perspicacious.

Matter lets spirit shine through. The flesh is an excellent vehicle for divinity. When Christ became incarnate, he chose among all human values those closest to divine values. He didn't choose poverty, meekness, suffering, failure, love, and obedience as so many alien ornaments that would attract people, but as human virtues that were also divine beatitudes. One may of course feel that this was true once, but that Christ *now* is back in heaven, and expects us to believe in him blindly. He is beyond our reach, and we can only feel a nostalgia for the time when the word was flesh. But no. Though Christ became invisible at the ascension, he keeps a voice, a body, a human presence among us: the church. God's method of intervening among us has remained so human and material that the apostles said of the Holy Ghost himself, when he came to found the church, that they saw and heard him (Acts 2:3). And he continues to be seen and heard throughout the church, 'for it has seemed good to the Holy Spirit and to us' (Acts 15:28).

Epiphany, incarnation, sacraments—all these, as Guardini has said, are constant necessities of christian life. God comes to us where we are in order to raise us to where he is.

That . . . which we have heard, which we have seen with our eyes, which we have looked upon and touched with our hands, concerning the word of life—the life was made manifest, and we saw it. [1 Jn 1 : 1f.]

The wonder expressed here by St John is the wonder at a permanent incarnation with which we are being invited to communicate in the sacraments and in love of our neighbour. A strange confusion of purpose seems to reign between ourselves and God. We long to leave the world behind—and God enters it. We yearn to cast off our crude outer shell of flesh, but God was made man and has remained so. We can only find him within. We are constantly lured by the hope that by becoming God we may cease to be men— weak, subject to temptation, suffering, and sin. Yet God affirms that it is possible to be at once God and man, and that his power is best manifested in our weakness.

Our religious aspirations are an extension of our childish dreams of escape, in which we imagine a life without suffering or sacrifice. After all, how can a human life with its failings and blemishes have anything to do with God? God's answer to this is not to change the conditions of our life, but to come and share them. The incarnation is an intensely sacred character conferred upon every moment of our existence, every person we meet: God in the commonplace, God in the routine and boring daily round, God so hidden that he could pass thirty years unnoticed in the world. So is God present now in the insignificant and useless scrap of bread, no different from the scraps we leave on the table after a meal, the scraps children throw away (despite all commands not to) when they've had enough. If our entire life is sacred, is consecrated by that once-for-all incarnation, then we must stop longing for any life other than this one in which God has come to join us. We must submit to being bound by our human condition, for he shares it with us.

No one who is baptised can doubt that the incarnation is permanent and progressive, and that it has given us the power in our turn to become children of God; and since God is incarnate today, it is precisely my life—or rather me—that he needs, an ordinary man, an ordinary life, an ordinary face. What the incarnation above all reveals is that we are so poor that the whole of God's love within us is not too much to help us begin to love husband, wife, children, parents, work, friends, as they need. One must be God to be able to love men. And, conversely, man must be God to give us a sufficient motive for loving him, to give us a reason proportionate to the immense sacrifices and terrible disappointments such a love involves. The only way to love man is to believe God is a man.

And here the incarnation reveals its everlasting wonder, which we shall never fully understand.

The incarnation didn't finish at Christ's ascension. Jesus remains man; a man who is seated at the right hand of the almighty Father. Furthermore, since the ascension, the incarnation has been extended. The hypostatic union of two natures in one divine person remains the privilege of Christ, the word of God. But there is a real union between every man and Christ through Christ's life being communicated to him. That union, though it leaves each man his own personality distinct from that of the divine person who vivifies him, is yet so close that God is really present and accessible in every man. 'To see your brother is to see Christ': to the eyes of faith, in other words, to eyes practised and far-seeing, Christ is present in the least of men.

In thirty-three years of life, Christ couldn't express all the divine love dwelling in him. He could only suffer in a certain number of ways, could only die once. 'Have pity on him', said Claudel, 'who had only thirty-three years to suffer in. Join your sufferings to his, for one can only die once.' Pity him, for he couldn't be a father or mother, an invalid, factory worker, or miner, an office-worker or urban slum-dweller, a displaced person or cripple. During his life he could only live in one state, ply one trade. Had we been able to see Christ living as we live, working at our job, we should have had a new understanding to apply to them. Had he been able to give an eternal value only to the few human things he made divine in those thirty-three years, then his death would indeed seem a terrible and ridiculous waste.

So short an incarnation would indeed be hard to understand. But he was made flesh once only because he was to be made flesh forever. Christ was born once because he was to go on being born for ever; he suffered once only because he was to go on suffering till the end of time. He died and rose once only because he was to die and rise for evermore.

Thus the incarnation is final. The redemption will always continue to operate through the same means with which it began—the body of Christ. Christ is still man today, not only because his glorified human nature sits at the right hand of the Father, but because it continues for ever being embodied in other men, who complete it. As von Balthasar has written:

> The historical life of the historical Christ and the historical life of the mystical Christ are thus not two distinct lives, but a single life under two aspects, the one symbolic and exemplary, the other symbolised and real. Never separate Christ and the church, for they are one flesh. [Hans Urs von Balthasar, *Recherches de sciences religieuses* 1936, 543f.]

We cannot come to God by any way more direct than the church— and that includes our brethren, the word (not a dead book, but the living proclamation of the word in the church), the sacraments (not acts of private devotion, but community celebrations), and prayer (awareness of Christ's life in and around us, and the working out of the 'communion of saints'). We mustn't separate love of God from love of man.

If you love the members of Jesus Christ, then you love Jesus Christ; in loving Jesus Christ, you are loving the Son of God, and in loving the Son of God you are by that very fact loving the Father. This love can admit of no division.

So wrote St Augustine. And St John Chrysostom:

Whoever accepts one of these two [precepts] is observing the other ... Neither a soul without a body, nor a body without a soul, can be a man. Similarly one cannot speak of charity to God without its going hand in hand with love of neighbour.

Have you noticed how, in the gospels, Christ commands us not so much to love him as to love one another—'that they may be one even as we are one' (Jn 17:22). He who came, not to be served, but to serve, continues in us to love others first. Christ is he who loves in us. We only know him in the movement by which we let him love and serve others in us—with the selfsame love of the Father who sent him. God only sees himself in us if we have become God towards others. 'We know that we have passed out of death into life, because we love the brethren' (1 Jn 3:14). In fact, one may wonder what was so new about the 'great commandment' Christ gave. After all, it had been in Leviticus for centuries: 'You shall love your neighbour as yourself' (Lev 19:18). The total renewal Christ has brought—the 'good news'—is the incarnation, whereby the second commandment has been made equal to the first. Now, by loving our brothers, we are loving God. God has given himself to man so totally as to become one with them. The duty of loving our neighbour—previously limited to mean parents, friends, neighbours, fellow countrymen—is henceforth extended to all mankind, for all are now a single family, a single people, a single man, a single body, in Christ. We shall not love them merely 'as ourselves', but as Christ loves them, letting his love be made flesh in us, loving them as we love him.

The irreconcilable enemy of the incarnation is the pharisee—the man who, under the pretext of zeal towards God, detests and condemns God-made-man. He thinks it is only a man he is hating; in fact, he has chosen to reject God himself. Pharisaism continues to exist in all those who try to make their rich relationship with God an excuse for their poor relationship with their fellow men. 'The hour is coming when whoever kills you will think he is offering service to God' (Jn 16:2). In our Lord's day, they had worked out a way of getting out of paying a living allowance to their parents by dedicating all their goods to God. You couldn't, after all, raid money consecrated to God to provide food! The fact that their accounts with God were in order gave them a clear conscience as regards their accounts with other people. Christ turned this idea upside down. He tells us that our account with God and our neighbour is one; we can be no closer to God than by being close to our neighbour. The only decisive proof that we love God is that we also love others. That is why I say that the most dangerous of all heresies is to disembody Christ, to think we can re-purify God from his body, and put him back in heaven; to think that this is how best to honour him.

With God safely in heaven, I can hate my neighbour undisturbed. Or rather, I can save myself even the trouble of hating him, and simply forget him, ignore him, and concentrate in tranquillity upon myself and my cosy Sunday religion; I can pay my respects to the almighty one day a week, and do what I like on the other six! Alas, there is no such peace to be found in the religion of the incarnation. There is only a permanent uneasiness, for God is here. 'I was hungry . . . I was thirsty . . . I was sick . . . I was in prison' (Mt 25:35f.). All our social structures are antichristian: capitalism, the proletariat, class privilege, money privileges, privileges of race and colour, privileges of education and culture, all privileges and barriers, for they indicate so many oppressions: and Christ is not among the privileged. Christ is in the world, and his presence is terrible. He lives here, and it is fearful to fall into the hands of the living God. Those who oppose the incarnation want a comfortable religion, leaving Christ out of it. Respectfully, of course, bowing to the blessed sacrament, thanking him for the trouble he has taken. Thirty years of suffering among us is more than we can cope with. We dispose of him in a cloud of incense, sending him into retirement, into a heavenly Taj Mahal. Then we can get on with the business of running the world—so much simpler when he is not there to interfere and complicate matters.

But it's impossible. Redemption always takes place through the incarnation. Christ is always a saviour, and he always saves us in the same way —by communicating with man, coming to carry our crosses, remaining with us all days even to the consummation of the world. And when that time comes, there will resound the same cry as resounded at the beginning: '[Cain,] where is Abel your brother?' (Gen 4:9). If you haven't honoured Christ in his members, then you have dishonoured the head. The last judgement won't bear upon our relationship with God, for that permits of too many illusions.

> Not every one who says to me, 'Lord, Lord,' shall enter the kingdom of heaven, but he who does the will of my Father who is in heaven. On that day many will say to me, 'Lord, Lord, did we not prophesy in your name, and cast out demons in your name, and do many mighty works in your name?' And then will I declare to them, 'I never knew you.' [Mt 7:21-3.]

God isn't concerned with what we do 'directly' for him. 'Then you will begin to say, "We ate and drank your presence, and you taught in our streets"'—we were regular churchgoers and communicants, and listened to innumerable sermons —'But he will say, "I tell you, I do not know where you come from"' (Lk 13:26f.). I was hungry, unhappy, ill, alone. I was a stranger, and you didn't take me in. I was helpless, and you gave me no word, no sign. I waited, and you never came to see me. You never paid us any heed when we had a birth, or a baptism, or a first communion in the family. You left us alone. You can stay alone now.

There is always a temptation to escape from the incarnation, to seek consolation in God for our failure to obey him, to seek his help in becoming resigned to not loving our fellows. St Matthew (25:31–46) makes clear what hypocrisy this is: here we find the great, surprising, stupefying novelty (the *new* commandment)—God has been made flesh, God has become man. The text opens in the majestic style of a heavenly religion:

> When the Son of man comes in his glory, and all the angels with him, then he will sit on his glorious throne. Before him will be gathered all the nations . . . Then the King will say to those at his right hand, 'Come, O blessed of my Father, inherit the kingdom prepared for you from the foundation of the world.' [Mt 25:31f, 34.]

This is all very lofty. But then it changes sharply to the harshest reality, with a kind of cold-water shock. What does this King say from this throne in the clouds?

> I was hungry and you gave me food, I was thirsty and you gave me drink, I was a stranger and you welcomed me, I was naked and you

clothed me, I was sick and you visited me, I was in prison and you came to me. [Mt 25: 35f.]

Religion 'up in the clouds' is succeeded by incarnate religion: God brings us back to earth. And most surprising of all, our Lord declares that religious teaching will always be the least important element—for neither the wicked nor the just were expecting to be judged by this yardstick. They hadn't been warned. They didn't know that the second commandment was equal to the first—they didn't know about the incarnation!

6
Born of the virgin Mary

Devotion to the Blessed Virgin has become a sore subject in christian spirituality today. It should be impossible to love the Father and not love Mary. She, too, could say to us: 'If God were your Father, you would love me, for I proceeded and came forth from God' (Jn 8:42). It should be equally impossible to love Mary and not love the Father. Yet alas both 'impossibilities' are constantly occurring, and those responsible for religious training must be ever on the watch against them. One is, of course, far worse than the other. Nothing can be more terrible than to forget the Father, to fail to pray to him or love him. Yet how many christians really believe that 'the Father himself loves us'? This—the worst error—is also the most natural for us to fall into. For man is more likely to become attached to a creature without rising from it to its Creator than the reverse.

That is why talking of Mary calls for special

prudence and discretion. At a time when the essentials of religion are so widely forgotten, our masses dead, our sacraments closed in, when scripture is so little known, the Holy Spirit forgotten and the Father left in the background, we must fight hard not to get carried along with the stream. Even though we have to talk to people at their own level and in a language they can understand, we must still be using it to lead them on to the esentials which they either do not know or have forgotten. All too often the cult of the Blessed Virgin and the saints increases in direct proportion to people's dechristianisation. When people find God too distant, Christ too divine, revelation unsatisfying, the Holy Spirit unhelpful, they hurl themselves into minor pieties and champion doubtful apparitions and private revelations. They move from the central to the peripheral. All those who find that God has not revealed himself fully enough in Christ, that God has not come close enough to us in Christ, that God does not do enough for us in Christ—all these are ripe for Antichrist.

Then too there are many who think they can get from our Lady and the saints things they cannot get from God. They feel closer to them than to Christ, and imagine that these intermediaries will understand and love them better than God will. As if anyone could be more gracious to us than our Father! As if any creature could understand us better than our Creator! As if Christ had not done enough to come close to us! Such devotion as this to Mary and the saints must be paid for by a parallel impoverishment in people's ideas of God. When these christians pray to the saints, they subtract those prayers from their prayers to God. They achieve the paradox of taking away from God what God gives unceasingly to his saints.

Books and sermons on our Lady seem to suffer from a tendency to hot air; to saying more than they think, and insinuating more than they say ('Mary is almost divine', 'Her power is almost unlimited', 'She attains to the fringe of divinity'). The thinking listener finds this kind of thing infuriating. Is the truth about Mary so poor that one can only praise her by exaggerating?

1. The intercession of the saints

It is important to keep making it clear that only God is God, to exalt his power and goodness as infinitely beyond those of all creatures. No one loves us more than the Father. There is nothing good in Mary and the saints that does not come entirely from God, nothing that is not to be found infinitely more glorious in God. But we must be careful when claiming all holiness, goodness, generosity, and the rest for God, not to end up by denying him the attribute of giving to others. If only God can give, then he gives nothing. If God gives nothing to his creatures that changes them, nothing they can radiate and pass on in their turn, then he has never given them anything. If God has taught us only to receive, then he has given us nothing of himself. For he *is* giving.

If God really wanted to communicate with us, he would have to do more than give; he would have to give us the power to give. His gifts must remain active and stimulating to action in us, must engender in us a likeness to the giver by leading us to give in our turn. God doesn't show his greatness by reserving to himself the prerogative of being a saviour to millions of isolated beings, all self-centred and incapable of communicating with each other. Far from it. He gives, but he gives the power to give. Only God calls, but he gives us the power to respond.

The church is a vast assembly of brethren in which one never receives a grace except to pass it on to someone else. God is the fount, but by drinking at him man becomes a fount in his turn:

> The water that I shall give him will become in him a spring of water welling up to eternal life. [Jn 4:14.]

God wants to let us taste the joy of God which is the joy of giving. He wants to let us be God in our turn. God has chosen to sanctify us through one another; he wants to need us. He takes no pride in being alone in loving, but only in making others love, extending that love, spreading it outwards with and through us. It is always easier to do a thing yourself than to get it done. The masterpiece of God's love is that it has drawn men into its current.

> The masterpiece of God's love is the Church.
> The masterpiece of the Church is the saints.
> And the masterpiece of sanctity is Mary.

What do the saints do in the order of grace? How do we act upon one another? What precisely do we expect our prayers to achieve?

Many people's ideas on this subject are completely pagan. Pagan prayer believes that it can change God's mind, by informing him, and making him fully aware of the state of a case to which he does not attach sufficient importance. Indeed it goes further, setting out to arouse a sleeping God, to touch the heart of an indifferent God, to improve an imperfect God, to make him favourable and attentive to our needs. The greater its supplications, the greater its blasphemy. True prayer, on the other hand, means at last letting God become God in us, being prepared for him to act in us, opening ourselves to his influence. Praying means finally letting God do in us what he has always wanted to do had we but given him the time and opportunity. It is God who prays and who loves in us—who inspires us to pray, and gives us so many gifts that we long to give too. Prayer is a supernatural activity:

> The Spirit helps us in our weakness; for we do not know how to pray as we ought, but the Spirit himself intercedes for us with sighs too deep for words. [Rom 8:26.]

God's plan for the salvation of the world requires our collaboration if it is to be carried out (cf. 1 Cor 3:7; 2 Cor 6:1).

Prayer means letting oneself be uplifted to ask of God what God wants to give; accepting to be for others what God wants to be for them through us. Only by identifying ourselves with the mind of God do we really pray well ('Whatever you ask *in my name*, I will do it', Jn 14:13). For prayer is precisely the act by which I stop speaking of myself ('my name', 'my kingdom', and above all 'my will') and speak, in the Son's name, of the Father's business: Thy name, thy kingdom, thy will . . . When I allow myself to be lifted up to God's level, then I begin to pray for others, then I become of some value in the order of salvation and charity. To intercede, then, is not to act as a go-between: when I pray for someone else, the pattern is not God-myself-another, but God-in-me. God-in-my-place, myself wholly invaded by the Spirit who, alone, in me, can say 'Abba, Father', who alone can effectively care for those for whom I have promised to pray. With grace there are no intermediaries—only collaborators. Instruments. Sacraments. Those to whom a saint lets God through, so to say, are touched by God himself.

Why then, the economy-minded will ask, if only God acts, don't we always go straight to God? Because only the infinite variety of the saints can show us the infinite variety of God's inventive goodness. We know God better for knowing the saints; we need them all to show us the riches of God's love. The saints 'complete what is lacking in Christ's afflictions' (Col 1:24). What things are lacking? Christ only lived one short human life of thirty-three years. He couldn't be a father or mother, a soldier or king, a district nurse or galley slave. But he can live all these states of life through those who are in them and who let themselves be invaded by him. Nothing of what we love in the saints but comes from God and was given them by God. What he has given them is an infinite variety of 'complementary humanities'. The story of the saints is always the story of what God can do in the lowliness and weakness of his servants. In his saints we see God.

2. Mary's intercession

Because Mary is the most faithful of all creatures, the most continually consenting, the most perfectly responding to God, she is also the most creative. Mary is a mother because God is Father; she was the creature in whom God was best able to show himself as Father. God has willed to need men, to depend upon us. His first and favourite dependence is his dependence upon Mary. He asked her to consent to be invaded and filled by God, to have nothing of her own any more—no plan, no future, no children, no husband—but to receive everything from him and give it back to others. Our Lady became simultaneously mother of God and of men, mother of the saviour and of the redemption. She is the mother of us all because she is the mother of Christ, whose members we are.

With the annunciation, Mary was the first to begin to receive Christ's body within her, the first to 'communicate'; she must have known a thousand times better than we that she was not welcoming him for herself alone, that she was not receiving him for her own sake, that she could never have him to *her*self because he would never belong to *him*self. By definition, the mother of the saviour was from the very first what the world calls a self-sacrificing mother. Her physical motherhood was a privilege. But her supernatural, universal motherhood is the most agonising mission ever set before any creature. She knew at once that she would have to accept to be mother of sorrows. Even during Jesus' childhood, he was not 'hers'; it wasn't she who taught him how to be a son, but he who taught her how to be a mother —and a daughter. When he was twelve, he taught her what obedience to the Father meant. The sword spoken of by Simeon was given its first thrust by her own Son.

Our Lord's apparent harshness to Mary in the gospel is striking indeed:

> His mother and his brothers stood outside, asking to speak to him. But he replied to the man who told him, 'Who is my mother . . .?' [Mt 12: 46-8.]
>
> Jesus said to her, 'O woman, what have you to do with me . . .?' [Jn 2:4.]

And so on. Some commentators have thought it better to soften the harshness of these episodes, but theirs is a superficial vision. A true understanding reveals the far more splendid fact that it indicates, not a failure, but a sure sign of the most perfect harmony between Jesus and Mary. He knew that he could ask this of her, that he had her unquestioning fidelity; in short he dared *not* to explain, or soften, *not* to smooth things over as others, more shortsighted, would demand. We can be most abrupt with those we love most. It is a mark of great affection when we can dare to treat others with the same liberty as ourselves. The closest communion, after all, is the one that least needs to be put into words. When Jesus looked at Mary he knew, without her having to say a word, that she believed. That certainly was his greatest joy and consolation in life. And the silence of the gospel about their relationship, far from being disturbing, is the most outstanding honour that could be paid to her.

It was at the foot of the cross that she became totally a mother, because it was there that she accepted most perfectly to give everything. She gave back to the Father the dearest thing she had, and—in the same gesture—gave him to the world. And giving him to the world, delivering her Son to the world, she made the world a world of sons, and gave the world to the Father. At that moment, agonisedly bringing us to life in the life of the Son she was giving us, she became fully our mother. All the 'privileges' she had received had been to lead up to that great *fiat*. She became the crown of humanity by this total consent; she is the supreme handmaid, for she accepted that everything should be done to her according to the word of the Lord. And her work goes on always. As long as the body of her Son is incomplete, her motherhood continues. Now, as in the past, she gives birth—in the joy of Bethlehem and the pain of Calvary.

3. Mediation

What does *mediation* mean? Everyone is agreed that there is only one mediator between us and the Father: Christ. St Paul (1 Tim 2:5) is too definite on this point for any doubt. Yet some describe Mary as our mediatrix with the Son—'apud Filium'. We have already seen how totally Christ's own words exclude the possibility of there being anyone *between* himself and us. One must say, therefore, that Mary exercises her mediation *with* the Son, in cooperation and harmony with him.

The phrases: 'To Mary through Jesus', 'To Jesus through Mary', are simply tautologies. Mary is not a route: 'Mary is not the intermediary', as Père Doncœur has put it, 'but the monstrance. The christian goes to the Father through the Son in the Holy Spirit. That is the order of things.' But the unity between Son and mother is too perfect, too total, for anyone to be able to see Jesus without Mary, for anyone to grow in Christ without simultaneously growing closer to Mary.

Honouring Mary is, therefore, the necessary fruit of our growth in incorporation into Christ. The more we become Christ's, the more attuned we grow to Mary, the more we must marvel at her existence. In this sense marian devotion isn't optional. If we don't feel the enthusiasm of sons for her, we aren't in harmony with her Son, we aren't in fact her Son's brothers, his members. By baptism we are incorporated into him: a life faithful to that baptism must give rise to real filial gratitude; and she, whose *fiat* made it possible for the word to be made flesh, will inspire the same gratitude and pride that Mary's love inspired in our Lord. Being made connatural with the Son, we will share his cares and affections, and above all, of course, his total accord with Mary. This is what 'To Mary through Jesus' would seem to mean.

In the same sense, and as part of one and the same movement, we must understand 'To Jesus through Mary'. Even more impossible is it to accept the idea that one could stop for a moment with Mary and not at once find oneself in Christ—for she is simply his perfectly adequate resting-place, his perfectly transparent tabernacle, the one who is perfectly 'changed into his likeness' (2 Cor 3:18). She isn't our mediatrix for reaching him, but a mediatrix through, with, and in him.

Abbé Moeller wrote that he considered the term *mediatrix* an ill-chosen one. I agree, for it is dangerously vague, and leads to ambiguities. If it is defined, it will certainly be with so many qualifications and fine distinctions as to make it mean something quite different from what first springs to mind. Meanwhile, the term *intercession* avoids the overtones of blasphemy that go with the term *mediation*—the suggestions of distance, of an intermediary, of some gap to be bridged between our Saviour and us. But *intercession* isn't really satisfying either. It, too, requires much explaining to make it mean what we want it to mean. Indeed, a lot of explaining is needed to bring people not only to a true idea about the saints, but to a proper devotion towards them, for few forms of piety turn so easily into superstition. The less believing the age, the greater the minor devotions. At a time when faith is alive even the most naïve religious practices are living and breathing, lifted to the level of reality by the vigour of people's belief. But when religion weakens, these little devotions are like blood vessels grown dry: sclerosis sets in, and then deterioration. The weakening of faith in our day could thus turn genuine devotions into superstitions. When we have so little faith we must concentrate on essentials only.

I should like to explain my opposition to the term *mediatrix* by considering the mediation of Christ. The objection might be raised that if God who is our Father, and loves us more than anyone else could, has none the less established a mediator between himself and us, why rule out the possibility of a mediatrix between Christ and us? This objection springs from a failure to understand how Christ mediates. God made Christ mediator not to place someone between himself and us, but precisely to unite us to him. Christ is not an intermediary. The Father has not sent us a go-between: he has given us the best he has, and thus united us to him. He has associated us for ever with his Son, with him in whom he can best recognise himself, with him in whom he is wholly pleased.

The Father would have united us no more closely to him by becoming incarnate himself. Christ's mediation is not something interposed between God and us, but on the contrary the most intimate union we could possibly have with him. (If our Lady were mediatrix, she would be something interposed, an intermediary. Only God unites to God. Only God is communicable to such a point. Christ is mediator because he is the Man-God.) And so we have an ontologically based solidarity with Christ whereby, whenever we let him do his work in us and ourselves consent to it, we are raised to the life of God.

And Mary, full of grace, a perfect window for God, completely docile, wholly possessed by God, lived that divine life always. She never ceased to be lifted up to the effective consent which we, poor sinners, approach from such a distance. Thus she reveals and gives God with all the intensity of a being totally invaded by him—the only being who has ever been so. She is the handmaid *of all graces*.

Historically, Mary comes before the church—at one point she was the whole church, the whole of consenting humanity, and by her assumption she is already all that the church will one day be. People have rightly called her the 'eschatological ikon of the church'. But she surpasses the church in the majesty of her maternal privilege; by it she was able to be the first to cooperate in the redemption, and at one moment was alone in receiving it, with a total consent impaired by no hesitation, no hint of withdrawal. From the moment of her immaculate conception she was wholly God's; she remained so until the assumption which brought her back to God again; and she spent her life in a permanent act of consent which made her truly God's daughter, and therefore truly the mother of mankind.

In this way 'To Jesus through Mary' takes on a

new meaning, secondary but perfectly real. Secondary, because we are first of all, by baptism, incorporated *into Christ*; but real, for in effect we, like Mary, must give birth, arouse, manifest Christ and make him grow. Every one of us is called to this supremely maternal function. We too are called upon to bring him into the world, to make him flesh—our flesh—to lend him our hands, our eyes, our faces, our mouths to speak through, our hearts to help and console. And Mary is actively our mother, for it is her special grace to give birth to us as beings who do this. It is from Mary that we receive this openness to the life-giving action of the Holy Spirit.

7
Suffered under Pontius Pilate

What exactly is the redemption? Do we think of it as the paying of a ransom? Why did the Father send his Son? Just to suffer? There are those who think the Son's mission was to suffer, and 'pay' for sinners. But what was he paying? And to whom? And if he has suffered for us, why have we still got to suffer ourselves? What is this mysterious value, this strange necessity of suffering, so that Christ's mission was not to set us free from it, but lead us into it?

On this question, we flounder about in a mixture of mistakes and lies. 'We are involved in Adam's sin', we say with a sigh, feeling not the least sense of communion with Adam—that fool who made some false move in the shadows of prehistory and so landed us in all this trouble. Because of him we must pretend to feel distress and humiliation. Then, with an equally artificial joy, we turn the page, and cry: 'But Christ has saved us!' We didn't feel particularly 'lost', so the knowledge that we are saved does not stir us greatly. However, we know the motions: we give every appearance of feeling intense relief. And we start once more from scratch.

For what, in fact, is changed in our situation as a result of all this? We couldn't feel that we were 'sinners' because of Adam's sin, and Christ's redemption has done nothing to dispense us from suffering. God is 'appeased' by Christ's blood, so it seems. The match is a draw. There was a drama, but the whole thing was over before we came along; it has taken place without us. The pints of innocent blood required to pay the ransom of the captives has been worked out, and the matter has been comfortably settled. 'Since the offence was infinite, an infinite victim was needed', and so on. The Son's expiation was equal in importance to the Father's anger. This picture of the redemption is one we all have, more or less consciously, somewhere in our minds. And it is monstrous. The redemption was carried out *in* suffering. But must we believe that it was *by means of* that suffering? That is really the crux of the problem.

Our entire religious life is governed by our answer to that question. Far too many christians still think suffering has some value in itself. Why, in that case, didn't Christ command us to make one another suffer? That would have been an easy precept. He could have said, not: 'Love one another', but: 'Mortify one another'. The redemption was achieved by a sacrifice. But what precisely is a sacrifice? Few words have been so de-natured. 'No sacrifice is too great for us'; 'I make a daily sacrifice for my spiritual bouquet. I haven't made enough for this week yet'—and the child puts a pebble into his sock as the last petal to make up his bouquet for God!

Sacrifice no more means 'choosing something bad for us to please God' than it means cut-price selling. Sacrifice means to do something sacred (*sacrum facere*), to make sacred, to make something God's, to consecrate. Yet we translate it to mean loss, deprivation, destruction! To sacrifice a thing is to give it its utmost value, to divinise it; it is to create love, to love more, to reverence more. We can do no more to show our love for anything than sacrifice it. Sacrifice is the most happy and 'profitable' action in the world. Yet with the frightened egoism which clings to inessentials all the time, we think more of the loss than the gain. For when any creature—a thing, a privilege, a pleasure, an activity, or a person—is sacrificed, it 'loses' its profane character.

Every sacrament is a sacrifice. Baptism for instance, means consecrating, sacrificing, a child. It is a sacrifice for it makes something sacred. By baptism, your child passes out of the world of sin into the communion of saints. Incorporated into Christ, he receives from him a life that is everlasting, and worth infinitely more than the life you have given him. From now on he belongs more to Christ than to you. He lives Christ's life more than yours. Don't complain, 'He isn't just mine any more. How sad!' This child has become a sacred being. You should be glad, and bow before him.

Adore him, for he is a living tabernacle in your home.

Marriage is a sacrifice (and not just in the comedian's sense). All married couples are well aware that something essential is missing in their love and their promises if these remain merely profane—if they aren't made something sacred, a sacrament. And, just as at the marriage feast of Cana Christ changed the water, which was all the couple in their poverty had left, into wine, so they beg him to change their human and profane love into his own. At their marriage, husband sacrifices wife and wife husband. From then on, Christ joins in their love: 'That they . . . may be one . . . *in us*' (Jn 17:21), so that they can love each other as he loves them; for, left to themselves, they cannot really love one another at all. Marriage, the sacrament of marriage, makes natural love 'pass' into the supernatural order (for, like every other sacrament, marriage is a 'passover'). Each partner sacrifices his selfishness, his pettiness, and his weakness —who is to say what he is *losing*? When someone enters the religious life, everyone marvels at all he is giving up. Yet surely it is dreadful to see a gift in terms of what renunciation it involves: one can hardly imagine a bride and groom enumerating all the 'opportunities', the advantages, the people they have given up in order to marry each other!

Between God and man, between God's love and man's self-love, between the world of light and the world of the prince of darkness, there is only one bridge, one communication, one possible passage or passover: sacrifice. Sacrifice is the great work of joy, the supreme act of sonship, the act whereby something profane becomes sacred, a lost soul finds himself again, the temporal becomes eternal, the defiled consecrated.

God created all things in love, that is to say, in unity. The devil is the divider—dividing man from God, husband from wife (though he had welcomed Eve with joy, how meanly Adam blamed her, how horribly he dissociated himself from her after his sin!), nature from its master, man from his own body (he was ashamed, and no longer recognised it as himself), children among themselves (Abel and Cain), children and parents (Noah and his sons), the nations who no longer understood each other (Babel), all men—separated from each other by barriers of race, class, culture, or money.

The redemption is the re-union, the union of sons with the Son, of men who have once again become sons to their heavenly Father, men who have once again become brothers to their brothers on earth: through Jesus Christ, 'the first-born of many brethren' (Rom 8 : 29). God's wish is 'that they may be one'—we must get rid of our divisions —'as we are one': the only unity possible to us is the unity of God himself. We must 'sacrifice' ourselves.

Sin is repaired only by sacrifice. What should be a gift and a joy has become a restitution. But the happiness of returning is incomparably greater than any regret for what we are leaving behind. And the restoration is so complete that it re-awakens the innocence and integrity of our beginnings. Sacrifice is first and foremost an act of joy:

> I do as the Father has commanded me, so that the world may know that I love the Father. Rise, let us go hence. [Jn 14:21.]

The redemption is wholly a work of love—a work of love on the part of the Father who, far from demanding a ransom of suffering from us, so loves us that he sends his own Son to bring us back to him. A work of love on the part of the Son, who reveals himself to us not because he suffers, but because he loves. He reveals to us the love we have lost, and he communicates that love to all who open themselves to it. A work of love on the part of mankind who, once more become sons, love their Father and their brethren with all the love with which they are themselves loved. But it is precisely *because* the redemption is a work of love that it took place in suffering. Fidelity of love must inevitably bring about suffering. Christ on the cross represents total fidelity, total obedience. He did not seek that horrible suffering, but fought against it. Only his love for his Father and dedication to the mission he had received brought him to Calvary. The magnificence of Christ's passion lies in the fact that it was not an act of asceticism, a planned mortification, a wished-for mutilation, but simply love being faithful.

Do you wish to 'unite yourself to Christ's sufferings'? Then unite yourself to his love! Don't try to suffer more, but to love more—indeed, if suffering be the criterion, one should love less, for that would make everything far more painful and therefore (presumably) more meritorious! Love is far healthier, and just as effective: we should seek, not the effect (suffering), but the cause (which is the love that seeks the good of others, not one's own pain). 'But love tends to imitation', say the propagandists of suffering. Yes: but Christ didn't want or seek the cross. He wanted to love and obey, and the cross was 'added unto him'. If you seek for crosses in order to be like him, then you are doing the precise opposite of what he did.

Love, for man, is at once the loveliest and most terrible thing in the world. Created and formed for love, he has made himself incapable of it. Of course, he still remembers his destiny: he feels stirrings of love, impulses, beginnings. Anatole France says with terrifying cynicism: 'In love only the beginnings are delightful. That is why we keep on beginning again.' For any love that lasts must always cost a lot. Every love begins with an intoxicating period when two selfishnesses come together. Each feels as much pleasure as the other in being together, in giving what is asked, and receiving what is given. But this honeymoon period is short. We soon find out that to give ourselves means to lose ourselves; that to do someone else's will means to renounce one's own; to belong to someone else means no longer to be one's own master; and that love means self-sacrifice. It means self-sacrifice in the noblest sense—learning fidelity, true love, a deepening of one's character, a summoning of one's best qualities, liberation from the selfishness that will not give and the pride that cannot receive. But such a liberation cannot take place without pain, for we have become so wedded to our disadvantages. Anyone truly living in love has a sense of dying, losing himself, resigning his common sense, being cut off from his background and family and all that spells security. We are so weighed down, so embedded in the world, so turned in upon ourselves, that we can only be set free by being torn away.

God exists only in the gift of Father to Son and Son to Father. Whereas when we turn outwards towards anyone else, we have precisely the opposite feeling; there seems to be nothing of ourselves left! This explains Adam's sin: a fear to entrust himself, a fear of believing, of putting his trust in someone else, a fear of loving. And his sin has been ratified and repeated millions of times by us all; it impregnates our civilisation, is embodied in our social structures, advertised in our literature, made law by our codes. It has become second nature to us not to love, and we prefer it that way. Thus all our acquired dispositions must be turned upside down if we are to find once again our first vocation.

We also, when we set out to love, in other words, to enter the interests, the views, the life of someone else, we are thoroughly shaken up; we think we are losing our life and our soul, whereas we are simply learning to love as God loves. It is hardly surprising that we can only enter this new life with a certain dislocation. If one could make a hunchback straighten up, he would certainly feel as though his bones were being pulled apart.

We are attempting a transformation, a transfiguration. And we discover that before being transformed we must lose our old form; before being transfigured we must give up the appearance we have always had. It is hard. We always calculate the loss and gain, what we have in hand and what we are promised, the security and the risk. We are mistrustful and afraid.

Christ is the innocent, with neither selfishness nor self-love, wholly occupied with another's affairs, wholly given to those who need him, and given with love, even to the hands of his executioners. For thus is God's love expressed in the human situation; Christ was crucified, not because he wanted to suffer, but because he had truly put on the human condition while remaining love. We shall be 'crucified with Christ' in proportion as we let ourselves be incorporated into this mystery. We shouldn't say that we shall be sanctified to the extent that we suffer, but that we shall suffer— joyfully—to the extent that we are sanctified.

Let us not, then, imagine Christ bowed down by his Father's anger, but rather imagine him sustained by love of his Father in spite of all the weight of our sins. Nor let us imagine a God punishing the innocent for the sins of the wicked, but rather a son who devotes all his enthusiasm to loving his Father in a nature that is rebellious and afraid.

Christ on the cross was doing the same as in heaven: loving. When he was crucified, Christ was simply accomplishing here, in his distant provinces, amid the tumult of the elements, what he does unceasingly in his own dwelling-place in glory and joy. He gave thanks, he gave himself into his Father's hands. For an instant, in the course of the ages, heaven was opened, and we could contemplate the eternal happiness of God, the intensity of his joy, the power of his love. Our names for this are crucifixion, passion, cross, sacrifice; what it really was was love and happiness.

Christ's mission was to communicate that love to us. We were not to be exempt from suffering, but our sufferings and death would become similar to his. Love makes God give, and it makes his creatures give back. The love with which we give ourselves back, entrust ourselves to him, shows that we know the love with which he gave himself. If one doesn't love, then one can't have known love; if we don't give, then we haven't received. We have received nothing from God, we have nothing divine in us, unless we have the gift of giving. For God is giving.

8
The third day he rose again

1. Resurrection and incarnation

St Paul defines a christian as a man who believes
in the resurrection of the flesh; and St John as a
man who confesses Christ as having come in the
flesh (cf. 1 Jn 4:2). The two are the same belief.
The resurrection and the incarnation are one and
the same mystery: the resurrection is the incarnation perpetuated, but in flesh that is incorruptible
and life-giving.

The resurrection is the 'reincarnation' of Christ.
By it he took flesh again—a spiritualised, invisible
flesh which we can see if he so wills, but which is
manifested supremely in the presence of others
who are incorporated into and nourished by it. 'I
am Jesus, whom you are persecuting' (Acts 9:5).
'Christ is risen in a mystical body', says the theologian Durrwell. The resurrection is the incarnation extended and communicated to us (just as
Bossuet said the church was Christ extended and

communicated). It is the final incarnation, and since it the history of the world has meant but one thing—the building up of the body of Christ in order that through him and with him all honour and glory be given to the Father.

In God's plan the incarnation is the only means to salvation. That is why it is permanent: no one can be saved without becoming a member of Christ. And the reason is obvious: man is saved if he can be united to God, participate in the (eternal) life and (infinite) happiness of God. To be saved is to find God. Through the incarnation man meets God so perfectly that he enters into him, that he is incorporated into the humanity which God took only to open it to us: 'that we may be made partakers of his divinity who deigned to become partaker of our humanity . . .'

But christians today do not really live by faith in the resurrection of the flesh; they believe more in the immortality of the soul than in the resurrection of the body. The narrowing of the word *flesh* (which at first meant the poverty of the whole man apart from God, and has now come to mean only the body), and the development of the theology of the survival of the soul after death, have cancelled out our interest in the resurrection of the body. Having managed very well without our bodies in the interval between the particular judgement and the general judgement, we feel that we shall finally get them back as an honourable—but somewhat cumbersome—extra. This diminishes our estimation of Christ's redemption. Since our souls did not need him to survive, Christ's work, and his promise, are easily boiled down, if one doesn't stop to think, to the resurrection of—well, meat really. Not very exciting.

On the other hand, our christian of today, having made his notion of survival so spiritual that it is hard to imagine it at all (what kind of life can a disembodied soul possibly lead?), ends up by scarcely wanting it at all. As Guardini says, 'a purely spiritual immortality leaves us cold'. He is back in the state of those primitive peoples—the Jews included—who believe in a wraithlike, anaemic existence after death. As Homer put it: 'I would rather live on earth as another man's slave, even if he had little land and only few goods, than sit on a throne among the dead'—and he called them 'weak heads'.

How many believers in fact think of eternal life without some such apprehensions? They are the price we pay for having drifted away from the vigorous reality of the resurrection of the flesh.

The gospel does not speak of the immortality of the soul, for it is man as a whole to whom Christ promises a blessed eternity. He have hope in the future world only because of him. 'If for this life only we have hoped in Christ, we are of all men most to be pitied' (1 Cor 15:19).

2. Witnesses

Unlike ours, the apostles' preaching centred on the resurrection. It was for proclaiming it that they were persecuted: 'The priests and the captain of the temple and the Sadducees came upon them, annoyed because they were teaching the people and proclaiming in Jesus the resurrection of the dead' (Acts 4:1f.). They considered that the whole of their mission was to be witnesses of the resurrection. (Are we witnesses of Christ's resurrection? There is no apostolate apart from this witness!)

This Jesus God raised up, and of that we all are witnesses. [Acts 2:32.]

[You] killed the Author of life, whom God raised from the dead. To this we are witnesses. [Acts 3:15.]

When they were arrested and brought before the Sanhedrin, they replied firmly:

We must obey God rather than men. The God of our fathers raised Jesus whom you killed . . . And we are witnesses to these things, and so is the Holy Spirit whom God has given to those who obey him. [Acts 5:29f, 32.]

For St Paul, the essence of the christian faith consists in believing in the resurrection of the dead:

If the dead are not raised, then Christ has not been raised. If Christ has not been raised, your faith is futile. [1 Cor 15:16f.]

He even characterises the Jews as infidels, despite their fanatical monotheism, because they refuse to believe that God raises the dead; for the God who does that is the only true God.

Christ had explained to the disciples at Emmaus

that his resurrection had been prophesied in the scriptures:

'Was it not necessary that the Christ should suffer these things and enter into his glory?' And beginning with Moses and all the prophets, he interpreted to them in all the scriptures the things concerning himself. [Lk 24:26f.]

Paul, too, declares 'that he was raised on the third day in accordance with the scriptures' (1 Cor 15:4).

What are these 'scriptures'? Just Isaiah, and the few scattered verses of the Psalms that Peter quotes in his first discourse in Acts (2:25-8, 34f.)? Surely the reference is more to sacred history as a whole: death, burial, and resurrection is a pattern which is constantly repeated throughout the adventures of God's people. There is the creation, the fall, the promise of a saviour; the multiplication of mankind, their depravity and the flood, the saving of Noah; then idolatry becomes widespread, God chooses out Abraham; Esau becomes bogged down in material things (a mess of pottage!), but Jacob believes in the blessing, and gradually becomes Israel. Then, in Egypt, once again there is the pattern of prosperity, persecution, and then deliverance. It is the same in the promised land, and all the trials and exiles end up with joyful returns. The work of faith will always be to believe in danger when things seem to be going too well, and in salvation when things appear hopeless. Faith is always waiting for death and resurrection.

3. Relevance

Christ's resurrection is of importance to us because it is ours: 'if there is no resurrection of the dead, then Christ has not been raised' (1 Cor 15:13). It is in Jesus that we are called to eternal life, because we are a part of him (so much so that commentators on St Paul have some difficulty in explaining the resurrection of the wicked, for the only cause for resurrection given by St Paul is our incorporation into Christ).

Christ's resurrection is capital. Not because it is a decisive proof or astounding miracle. As apologetics, the raising of the widow of Naim's son, or Jairus' daughter, or Lazarus, are far more powerful, since they took place in public, in the presence of numerous witnesses, many of whom were unbelievers. But Christ's resurrection is important because it concerns us all, it touches each of us personally even now, in the twentieth century. It is a promise of resurrection to every man coming into this world. Christ's resurrection is capital because by it Christ enters his glory *at the head of all mankind*. In fact,

> As in Adam all die, so also in Christ shall all be made alive. But each in his own order: Christ the first fruits, then ... those who belong to Christ. [1 Cor 15:22f.]

The historical fact of Christ's resurrection is but the beginning of this permanent fact of our resurrection in him. What matters is not that Christ *has* risen, but that he *is* risen, that he is alive, that he

106

has fulfilled his promise to rebuild his body, the true temple, in three days—out of living stones, and with dimensions in proportion to his will to save. He *is* the resurrection. That Christ had risen would be of no interest to me unless he could rise in me; what difference would it make to me that he had emerged alive from the tomb, if he did not emerge gloriously from the darkness of my soul? It would be of little use his having appeared to the apostles if he did not manifest himself to me!

4. The risen body of Christ

Obviously the state of the risen body is different from that of our bodies. It would seem as if matter as we know it is in a state of degradation—that sin has made us heavier, more encumbered, so to say, than it is our nature to be. Paul uses the surprising phrase 'spiritual body'. It isn't a contradiction, for *spirit* doesn't mean *soul* (which, in biblical language, is as much 'flesh' as body is), but *Spirit of God*—Christ becoming 'life-giving Spirit', with the ability to transform all human reality and adapt it to a higher life. The body remains material, otherwise it would cease to be a body. But glorified bodies do seem to bring into question some of the essential qualities of matter. The risen Christ made himself visible and invisible at will—though he passed through closed doors, he could be touched, and he ate. The risen body seems to be characterised by being a docile instrument of the spirit. No longer slowing it down or localising it narrowly, no longer a barrier, it has become a perfect means of communication. Once risen, Jesus could come back to all those he loved easily, directly, and at will. He could be present any time, anywhere. 'May the body of Christ keep thy *soul* . . .' we used to say before communion: Christ's spiritualised body is the only means of salvation.

Left to itself, the 'flesh is of no avail' (Jn 6 : 63), but equally, brought to life by the Spirit, it becomes capable of being used for the most divine purposes. As things are, it does more to isolate us than help us to communicate; it makes us impenetrable by enabling us to conceal or dissemble our thoughts. 'The sense of solitude', said Mounier, 'is the awareness of all that has not yet been spiritualised in us.' The risen flesh of Christ is an unbounded principle of communion.

At his resurrection, Christ did not simply roll away the stone from his tomb; he abolished all the barriers enclosing us in our prisons in this life—of class, of race, of language, of time, of place and distance, and of sex:

> There is neither Jew nor Greek, there is neither slave nor free, there is neither male nor female; for you are all one in Christ Jesus. [Gal 3 : 28.]

And not only this, but he has even removed the barrier between this world and the next. His body, now extendable, communicable, and communiable, is the point linking the whole universe.

We should long impatiently, not for matter to disappear (for it makes us what we are), but for it to become supple, free, assumed into heaven.

We look forward to the spiritualising of our bodies. The difference between a shellfish and a skylark is no greater than the difference between the two ways of existing in the body. Our present capacities are at the shellfish level, limited by time, space, and fatigue; we are heavy, slow to understand, quick to drift apart from one another. Being cowards, we are resigned to this heaviness; so much so, that when we come to suffering, old age, and death, which is the first step towards improving things, we get the impression that we are losing everything. Our relationships are so poor, so tenuous, that we dare not hope to be given them back a hundredfold in our risen flesh.

When St Paul makes us speak of 'our heavenly dwelling' (2 Cor 5:2) we have a feeling that really to believe in it and long for it involves a kind of sensibility, a terrible renunciation of all that is beautiful in the world. 'A foretaste of death'? Yes, but of the victory-death which Christ's resurrection has made ours for ever, death with survival, or 'super-death':

> But our commonwealth is in heaven, and from it we await a Saviour, the Lord Jesus Christ, who will change our lowly body, by the power which enables him even to subject all things to himself. [Phil 3:20f.]

5. The means to this end

Our participation in the resurrection takes place, is renewed, and is intensified by the sacraments.

The more Christ becomes alive in us, the more his resurrection becomes ours. It is the function of the sacraments to effect in us what they bring to mind, what they re-present of Christ's life. In one sense, our life has already been lived in Christ and our lot settled; the creed recited at our baptism contains the whole thing: conceived by the Holy Ghost, born of the virgin Mary, suffered, died and buried, risen, ascended into heaven. We have no destiny other than Christ's. And Christ's whole existence is contained in the sacraments. 'Since Christ is no longer visible amongst us, all that is manifest of him has passed into the sacraments' (St Leo). The sacraments are Christ's body reaching out to us for us to see, touch, hear, receive, and let ourselves be transformed into him and by him.

Do you not know that all of us who have been baptised into Christ Jesus were baptised into his death? We were buried therefore with him by baptism into death, so that as Christ was raised from the dead by the glory of the Father, we too might walk in newness of life. [Rom 6:3f.]

Christ's passion is not complete unless we unite our sufferings with his. He is not truly dead unless we are dead with him. And what would be the point of his resurrection, if we did not rise with him? (cf. Acts 3:26 which reads in *The Jerusalem Bible*: 'It was for you in the first place that God raised up his servant').

Every sacrament is precisely this kind of participation in the death and resurrection of Christ. Baptism incorporates us into Christ that we may die with his death and rise in his resurrection. We may perhaps regret that our present liturgy has so diminished the sensible sign of the sacrament that its meaning is not clear. The trickling of a few drops of water on the person's forehead isn't enough to remind us that baptism is a passage through the Red Sea that drowns and saves, a bathing in the Jordan whence God's Son came out among sinners, and a figure of the still greater baptism of blood which Christ underwent on the cross. ('I have a baptism to be baptised with; and how I am constrained until it is accomplished!' Lk 12:50.)

Confession renews baptism by presenting another chance of dying—of getting rid of one's former self, that deadweight, mediocre character, so tedious to others, so insupportable to oneself. To die one need only enter the confessional. There we die to the poor, miserable, weak acts of self-will that are our sins; and we rise again to the will of God, which is love, faith, sincerity, righteousness, and hope.

The mass is essentially a participation in Christ's death and resurrection. Here again one may deplore the fact that our liturgy today puts all its emphasis on the real presence—so much so indeed that mass often seems more like a glorified benediction, with the elevation as its high point—instead of signifying more clearly 'the mystery of the passion, resurrection, and ascension'. Yet all the meaning is there: the mass is the true 'imitation of Christ', the surest way of patterning ourselves upon him, of joining ourselves to his life and death. Through it, we enter in obedience into Christ's total devotion to his Father. In it we become sons, brothers, and food in our turn, sacrificed and consecrated bread, bread which loses itself to become living bread. We communicate in a body that has been given, and blood that has been shed. That body begins to be given afresh in us; that blood becomes, in whoever receives it, a spring, a gushing fountain. It leads us to pour out upon others in our turn the blood that has been poured out for us.

To communicate is to eat the spiritualised flesh of Christ so as to make our own his power of resurrection. So much so that St Paul found it astonishing that a christian could become ill or die after having eaten this bread of everlasting life. He could only explain it by unworthy communions. Christ's body becomes so totally one with ours as to make us all one body living forever. We celebrate the eucharist 'until he comes' (1 Cor 11:26); surely, then, we are hastening his return by giving him our bodies to help his body to grow. Our last communion, the viaticum, will reveal the sincerity of all our others; only those of us who have become Christ's body by our communions are promised eternal life. 'The body of Christ keep thy soul [and body] to life everlasting.'

6. Witnessing to the resurrection today

The best proof that Christ is risen is that he is still alive. He gives life to us, and the only way the vast majority of our contemporaries can see that he lives is by seeing how we love one another. The only proof that Christ is still living is that love is still living on earth, *his* love, which was so great that he laid down his life for those he loved.

Christ has no visible body other than christians, and no other love to be seen but theirs. It is up to us to bear witness to his resurrection. 'It is a poor religion whose proofs are all in the past!' The fact that nowadays the masses are apostatising while intellectuals are being converted, is because now we can prove Christ's resurrection from books, from studying and research, which only intellectuals can undertake. The masses, the poor, the 'little ones', remain unconvinced. It should be enough for them to look and see—to look at us and see what we are; but they will hardly embrace the major sacrifices called for by conversion if all they will get out of it is to become like us!

It is for christians in every age to create the incarnation of Christ in their world, to make him present to their contemporaries. Every disciple of Christ is the brother and sister and mother of the Lord (Mk 3:35). Every christian must give him to the world, must enable him to be alive there once again, by lending him hands to make gestures of love with, a mouth to speak words of love with, a heart to radiate love to the world: 'where two or three are gathered in my name'—that is, are united, loving one another with Christ's love—'there am I in the midst of them' (Mt 18:20). Charity in the church, liturgical life that bears fruit, christian marriage, fervent religious communities, apostles (whether laymen or priests)—

all these are pledges and proofs of Christ's resurrection. The world, groping amid despair and doubt for the wounds of the risen Christ, needs to find in us the indubitable proofs of his living presence: an open heart, open hands, a loving and generous welcome. It needs to hear the gentle reproach Christ first made to Thomas: 'Have you believed because you have seen me?' (Jn 20:29).

The glory of the risen Christ is that he has created a new body for himself.

9
I believe in the Holy Ghost

Like all our great prayers, the creed is trinitarian. One sometimes forgets that the sign of the cross is an abridged version of the creed (a symbol of the symbol). By making the sign of the cross we affirm that we are going to act in honour of a paternal and creative love, by grace of a filial restitution, in a Spirit of love and mutual giving. It is a lot to think of all this in a single gesture—which is why most of us don't think about it at all. It is better to limit oneself to one idea—to act in the name of the Father, or of the Son, or of the Spirit; it makes concentration easier. Better still is to say the creed, which gives details and explanations, and transforms the simple gesture into contemplation.

1. His work

The whole of the third section of the creed is concerned with the Holy Ghost. We must beware of dividing into six separate articles this one last chapter of our faith. We should say, not: 'I believe first in the Holy Ghost, then in the holy Catholic Church, . . .', but, using a colon as punctuation: 'I believe in the Holy Ghost: in the holy Catholic Church, . . .'

All these works of the Spirit that we believe in, all his epiphanies which we list at the end of the creed—these are the *mirabilia dei* which the apostles were amazed at after Pentecost, and which Mary had glorified in in the magnificat. To recite (or still better, to sing) the end of the creed should mean a series of heartfelt exclamations, full of excitement, wonder, and gratitude. The earlier parts of the prayer have spoken of gifts and good things created for man by God, without mentioning the Holy Ghost, though he hovered over the waters of creation, spoke through the prophets, and overshadowed Mary. But the special work of the Spirit is the church. His indwelling there, as in his home, is as real as the incarnation.

The Spirit of God penetrates men, and his first effect in those who receive him is to gather them together, in a single new body. Because he is a Spirit of love and giving, who unites the Father to the Son and the Son to the Father, he makes us become like them. We become linked to one another by the same 'bond' that links the Trinity; we must henceforth treat each other with the love, the respect, and the devotion of the three divine persons for each other.

Like the humanity of Christ of which it is an extension, the church is 'conceived by the Holy

Ghost'; Pentecost is a continuation of the incarnation. The same creative Spirit which hovered over the waters in the beginning, which came down upon the Jordan at the start of Christ's mission, raises up the church daily from the waters of baptism. 'Thou shalt renew the face of the earth.' Every day, the Spirit renews the world, creates the church afresh by bathing it in the waters of cleansing. The historical incarnation is the vital point, but it would not by itself have been enough to save mankind. We need a continuing incarnation, for only God can teach us to love. We need a friend, a guide, a companion, a comforter. The only adequate homage we can offer the paraclete is to subscribe wholeheartedly to Christ's most astonishing statement: 'it is to your advantage that I go away' (Jn 16:7).

2. His personality

Who is the Holy Ghost? What distinguishes him from the other persons? And how is he united to them?

The easy answer is to say, 'It is a mystery'. But even a mystery must provoke some kind of idea in us; even in a mystery, there is something to understand. Indeed, it would be truer to say, there is *too much* to understand—our understanding will never be complete. It is not a matter of accepting that it is so, and then thinking no more about it; rather we must think about it enough to believe more and more deeply.

To understand something of the Spirit of God,

consider what is most precious and alive in a family—the family spirit. A family with no spirit is not a true family. But where there is family spirit, that spirit is something more real and more alive than any individual member of the family. All the members are marked and shaped by it, and whatever their differences, its presence can be felt wherever any of them go. One has only to meet one of them, to recognise at once, 'He is one of the so-and-so's'. One could never define in what it consists, this recognisable family air, but it is so real that all who have become sensitive to it will notice it on many occasions when others see nothing. This spirit is often stronger and more intense than the individuality of those who live by it. They are improved, enriched, given character, by belonging to this particular family.

What, then, is this spirit? It is a spirit of love that takes shape from the joyful, thoughtful, creative love that passes from parents to children, expressed in all manner of inventiveness, insights, generosity, sudden inspirations; and from the love that goes back from children to parents in respect, trust, admiration, pride, and joy. This exchange of its nature grows more intense. The more love comes down to the children from their parents, the greater the love the children will feel for them. And the more their children love them, the more will they love their children. It is a continual circulation and growth of love, so that finally, this family spirit becomes a person, a being distinct from the individuals who have brought it into existence.

From the mutual love of several people, a new reality has come into being, which at once contains and surpasses them all, draws them together and makes them radiate outwards, makes them a unity and yet intensifies the individual personality of each.

This gives us the best image we could have of the Spirit of God. He is love and the exchange of love between the Father and the Son. The Father turns towards the Son, and the Son towards the Father, with such power and joy that a person issues from them.

3. Mission

a. Filial Spirit

The Holy Spirit's mission flows from all that I have said about his person. He creates in us a filial spirit which incorporates us into Christ, and makes us turn to the Father crying, 'Abba! Father!' (Rom 8 : 15). Just as the Son's humanity was conceived by the Holy Ghost, so it is our being given the Spirit which places us in a truly filial condition.

Even in Adam the breath of divine life brought into being a creature in God's image, a son of God. But the wind of Pentecost created a new humanity, imbued with the Spirit of sons. The Spirit naturalises us, so to say, to the things of God. It gives us spontaneity, enthusiasm, a taste for and a spirit of the divine, to replace the law. Far from giving life, the law sterilises and kills. The pharisee was a man of law, with his passion for knowing the minutiae of what to do and what not to do. The rich young man kept the law, but did not recognise the Spirit of God. The Spirit, who is Father of the poor, master of those who listen, the revealer of the beatitudes, communicates the ways and tastes of God to us. Without him, we should have obligations but no enthusiasm, prayers but no inspiration—an insipid religion altogether. It is he who gives us a taste for the things of God: *recta sapere*—a savour, an interest, an appetite—so that insipidity vanishes. He gives us an interior understanding of what the church tells us exteriorly.

Only those of the household are interested in knowing what is going on inside it. Outsiders have no feeling for it. But the children are interested in everything to do with their Father. Unless we have the Spirit of adoption, the things of God will have no interest for us; they will mean nothing to us. The Spirit of sons will make us love the Father as Christ did, pray as Christ did, trust him with the same trust as Christ:

> [Father,] I knew that thou hearest me always.
> [Jn 11:42.]
> All mine are thine, and thine are mine.
> [Jn 17:10.]

These sound bold prayers, but they come irresistibly from a Son's heart.

By the Spirit, we dare to hope not only for salvation, but for joy. Blessed are they that suffer: in the Spirit this paradox becomes meaningful. The Spirit makes it possible to be happy on the cross, by being so fired with zeal for the Father. Flesh and blood are not sensitive to the things of God. But the gifts of the Spirit make us able to perceive, to experience, to savour them. By giving us the gift of loving God and our neighbour, he is letting us experience the love he himself loves with us: 'It is the Spirit himself bearing witness with our spirit that we are children of God' (Rom 8: 16). What matters is not to keep thinking about the Holy Ghost, but to follow his inspiration. It is good, however, to be aware that he is acting in us, and that the best way to honour him is to listen to what he tells us:

The Spirit of truth . . . will not speak on his own authority. [Jn 16:13.]

The Counsellor . . . , whom I shall send to you from the Father, even the Spirit of truth, who proceeds from the Father, . . . will bear witness to me. [Jn 15:26.]

The Counsellor, the Holy Spirit, . . . will teach you all things, and bring to your remembrance all that I have said to you. [Jn 14:26.]

b. Fraternal Spirit

But the Spirit cannot make us sons, without also making us brothers. We can't be in God without being in communion with our brothers. If it is true that where two or three are gathered in Christ's name—in his Spirit—, he is in their midst, then it is truer still to say that where Christ is, and his Spirit, there is union.

Jesus' supreme longing, 'that they may be one

as we are . . . that they may be one in us', was not merely for us to be united with him and the other divine persons, but, if you notice, first and foremost, to be united among ourselves. The Spirit of love, radiating from the Father to the Son, and the Son to the Father, also turns us one towards another. At Pentecost, he came down upon the apostles when they were gathered in one place, praying with one heart, forming one community of brothers. In us, too, he is the Spirit of communion. He gives life and shape to the body of Christ, not to isolated individuals.

The church is the Holy Ghost's epiphany. In her, he makes himself visible to many more than the three wise men—to the innumerable people who see the life of the church and marvel, 'See how they love one another'. The breath of the Spirit breaks stones and knocks down doors; it brings together total strangers, misanthropes, the shyest and the most hostile. How good it would be if he really blew upon us christians, in our churches on Sundays, on all the poor, cold people who seem hardly to be able to have faith at all, for they have never come in contact with the only reason for having it: they have never *seen* the Holy Ghost, they have never *seen* how people love one another. They simply do not know that Holy Spirit of mutual giving, of joy, of sharing and brotherly community.

Imagine a lot of guests coming to dinner, but not eating anything. Think of the hostess' horror as each one says: 'Do forgive me. I am delighted to be here, but really I'm not hungry.' And suppose a large number sat down with empty plates in front of them: 'We won't eat. We have simply come to please you.' Can you imagine anything more sinister or hateful than such a meal, or any behaviour more intolerable? One would take great pleasure in throwing them out, or at least in giving them a good shake, and saying, 'You wretched man, we haven't asked you to eat because you are hungry, but from sociability, to make an act of communion with us, to come together and share.'

Yet sadly enough, christians pour into church on Sundays with no appetite, determined to be excommunicated. The Spirit of love, of exchange, of brotherhood, of communion is absent from them. 'Do not quench the Spirit' (1 Thess 5:19), said St Paul; 'and do not grieve the Holy Spirit of God' (Eph 4:30).

Despite Vatican II's *Constitution on the Sacred Liturgy*, mass in most of our parishes is reminiscent of Ezekiel's prophecy about the dry bones. 'And lo, they were very dry' (Ezek 37:2). Or a modern tower of Babel, in which a confusion of tongues, as between priest and people, and between English and Latin, makes it difficult to act in unity. We need a true Pentecost, to hear with joy 'each of us in his own native language' (Acts 2:8)—and, more important, for this is no mere question of linguistic cleverness, for a miracle of charity to change us so that every person feels himself loved, understood, happy, united. 'You do not know what manner of spirit you are of' (Lk 9:55, in some texts), said Christ. And his own Spirit is the one who will make us turn joy-fully towards others. This does, indeed, involve something like a new creation—but, then, the Spirit is creative. 'Veni Creator Spiritus,' we say; 'Send forth thy Spirit and they shall be created, and thou shalt renew the face of the earth', the church prays with unshakeable optimism.

4. Creating Spirit

The real atheist is not the man who says, 'God doesn't exist'; he is the man who believes that God isn't capable of changing him, who denies God's power to transform, the infinite power of the Holy Ghost to create and renew. It is true atheism to claim, 'At my age one doesn't change any more' (and this can be said at fifteen or at sixty!)—to think oneself too old, too weak, too hardened; to think that one has tried everything, and that in one's particular case there is nothing to be done.

The Spirit is creative because true love is crea-tive. A great many people confuse love with a kind of bargaining. 'You give me something? I will give you something. You are smiling at me? I will smile too. If you give me no greeting, then I shall give you none. You give me no sign, and I'll not stir either.' It is all giving 'by rule'. Such a conception of human relationships brings about those situations of deadlock which seem so often to befall us even with people we are by way of loving.

The person who loves even when he isn't loved, who gives a greeting even when he is offered

124

none—he is creating something fresh, breaking up the deadlocks. He proceeds from a creative spirit. The love of parents for their children is of this kind; it is true love, the kind of love that is God's. Parents aren't devoted to their children because they are good or grateful, but because they want to make them so. And when a child is sullen, or obstinate, or difficult, they don't love him any the less for that. They never lose heart. 'I'll love him so much, forgive him so often—I'll suffer because of him and for him so patiently that in the end he'll be won over by my love and capitulate. In the end we shall understand each other.'

If we can behave like this with our children, why can we so rarely do so with others—our neighbours, our colleagues, our friends? If we could only love them all in this way, the world would be saved. For love like this creates more love. Such creative activity of the Spirit can be seen throughout the bible. In the creation, the Spirit hovered over the waters, and the world rose out of chaos, alive with freshness and beauty. At the flood, though it looked like the end of everything, things were wiped out only to be begun again; and a dove once again flew over this·new creation. At Jesus' baptism, the same sign came to indicate that at every baptism the Spirit would generate a new creature, to be greeted again with the great cry of joy from the Father: 'This is my beloved son, my beloved daughter.' And even after baptism, whatever may have been our failures and resistances, the Spirit will always be able to bring alive again in us that new son or daughter in whom the Father is well pleased.

The only face upon which God wishes henceforward to make the light of the Holy Spirit shine is ours. And not directly upon us, but upon those whom we have loved, cheered, enlightened, drawn together; those whom we have consoled. The comforter is revealed through those we have been able to comfort. And anyone who can't be comforted by seeing him thus, can't be comforted at all.

'Where two or three are gathered in my name, there am I . . . ' (Mt 18:20). Whenever anyone sees two or three who really love one another, he is seeing God; God is being revealed to him. The only evidence of the presence of God's Spirit among us is our brotherliness—there we can 'taste' the Spirit. For God is love, exchange, self-abandonment, mutual trust, the joy of being one in many. Brotherhood.

Those who are impervious to God's revelation in the life of the church will be given nothing more to believe. It is no use waiting for another revelation after that of the Holy Spirit, for there is no fourth person in the Trinity. To wait for anything further is to wait for Antichrist—and we have seen something of him in every generation.

If we look for an efficient but loveless organisation which will create a better world and give peace and happiness, or which will solve all the problems of technology and world-organisation, then we are the prophets of Antichrist. Whoever does not believe that only love can change the world is sinning against the Holy Spirit. He is losing the last gift, the for-giving of God.

10
The holy catholic church

The Holy Ghost, which we 'see and hear' (Acts 2:33) in the whole world, until the end of time, is the church. It is his epiphany, the place where he manifests himself through his work of union, of holiness, and of love. The church is one, catholic, and apostolic for the same reason that it is holy: because it lives by the life of God, which is a life of love. When the church is full of love it remains one, open to all, faithful to its bridegroom. It is the failing of charity which brings about divisions, narrowness, rebellions, through disobedience to the Holy Spirit of love.

The Holy Spirit's work is to convert the world, by bearing witness through the ecclesial community to God's love for the world. What Christ, who was conceived by the Holy Ghost, started when he was on earth, the Spirit continues and extends by bringing forth for him a body that matches his own love—universal and everlasting. Christ has no successor—not even a deputy or representative, as is sometimes wrongly suggested. He lives now. He always has a body, and when that body acts as itself, then it is Christ himself who acts.

The christian apostolate is to show the Spirit, to make him visible by giving him a body. The only way our contemporaries can look upon Christ's face is to see it in our communities of love. There is only one apologetic argument that is adequate to the world's need of faith, and that is a true and living church. The world will only be converted by seeing the miracle of people who truly love one another.

Our age suffers dreadfully from divisions: it is torn apart by human hatreds that increase as fast as distances diminish. Our economy today, like our wars, is on a worldwide scale. We are inextricably bound together, and yet the tragedy is that we do not love one another. We are united without love; we are drawn together by fear, by self-interest, by necessity. But we are not united by trust, by mutual help or faith. The world of today is organised like a single vast body, but it is a body inhabited by frightened little souls, hostile, vindictive, cowardly, unable to give it life, powerless to make its heart beat. The miracle it seeks from us christians, the miracle that will convert it, the miracle it needs—as the disciples needed wine, the Samaritan woman needed living water, the multitudes needed the loaves and fishes—is the miracle of our charity, a miracle of bold, active, joyous, self-communicating love. Wherever a christian lives, wherever a christian comes on the scene, there should be a community brought into being, a breaking of the ice; there should be a radiating joy, a sensitive and watchful generosity, a contagious devotion and self-forgetfulness. To this world that has become so small and so crowded, with people all irritating and disliking each other, we can and we must bring love, the power of communion, the food of the sacrament in which there is one bread shared by a vast multitude.

The world has never been closer to conversion, for the need for love has never been so apparent. Yet it has never been further, either, for the church has disappointed the hopes the world had placed in it. It criticises the church with all the force of the love it wanted to love it with— reproaches it for being so dead, so turned in upon itself, for defending itself as one party against others, for claiming to be so different, and yet being so exactly like all the others.

The reason why most of the young people whom we have educated, instructed, and catechised lose their faith is that they have never had this decisive proof, this argument that alone could fill their needs, the only evidence which could bypass all the arguments of apologetics: they have never seen the church. Of course they have *been* to church—oftener than they wanted, oftener than they needed. But there, above all, they did not find the church, they did not see that miracle which is not merely the proof, but far more important, the object of their faith: a community of adults who have learnt to love one another; Christ living in the assembly of his members.

We pity the 'church of silence', which we situate behind the iron curtain, or the bamboo curtain, or some other curtain. 'The wicked' are always other people. 'You hypocrite, first take the log out of your own eye' (Mt 7 : 5): we don't see that other curtain of indifference, of inertia, of happy ignorance, that makes us and our church (our parish, our group, our family even) a petrified church, a sleeping church, a terribly silent church where there is no exchange, no communion, no warmth or joy in being together in Christ to save the world. The real church of silence is ours; ours is the church where no one speaks, no one acts, the church which says nothing—to us or to anyone else.

In the world of working people, if you want to find brotherliness, support, warmth, you go to neighbours, to workmates, to the pub—but never to church. Among the middle-class, those who think of themselves as christians move in two quite separate sets. They have a lively, bright, interesting world of friends whom they meet socially, at sporting or cultural events, or places of amusement. These are the people they invite to their homes, whose religion they never ask about, nor want to discuss. Then there is their other, christian world, which has nothing sociable, or young, or pleasant, or smart about it. They meet these people through their good works, but never ask them to the house. One could hardly imagine dining with the do-gooders; that *would* be jolly. To quote Julian Green: '. . . A few bigots who smell of solid piety from ten feet away. A few thin and lofty-looking women, with the disagreeable air appropriate to those certain of their own virtue.'

Their children have no trouble in choosing between these two worlds. They cannot be said to be turning away from Christ, for they have never seen him. Christ is life, light, joy, and love. He can hardly be in those dismal assemblies where no one speaks to you or looks at you. Where everything is so planned and formulated that no one has to do anything out of the way. They can hardly feel any obligation to attend when their absence could make no possible difference. No one looks pleased to be there; you only start to live again when you come out.

As long as we haven't created around our children a world of adults who love one another, then we have not shown them the church. Their baptism has not incorporated them into any body. Their communions have not taught them to share anything. Their confessions have not brought them back into a community of brothers. Worse still—these ceremonies may well have lulled them into a sense of being dispensed from seeking the truth. Their faith really has no object: they haven't been present at the resurrection of Christ. The proof that Christ has risen is that he is alive; and he is alive wherever men love one another with his love. The role of a living parish, of a community of brothers, is to reveal the glorious face of the risen Christ, to make Christ visible.

132

This visible body of Christ is built up by a sensible sign—baptism. Baptism is not an operation of individual salvation; it saves only by incorporating us into Christ, uniting us to others, removing us from a divided world without love to a church in which the Spirit of love breathes.

Sin—original and unceasingly renewed—is division, is what makes us ignore, hate, despise, exploit, and oppress one another. To snatch a child from these coils of paganism in which he is caught up from birth (from his 'origin') requires all the exorcisms of baptism. The poor little thing is not possessed by the devil, but we ourselves have already enmeshed him in a devilish net of prejudices, divisions, and organised selfishness which will affect his entire life. It would require some mighty exorcisms to stop us belonging more to our social class than our religious community, to stop us feeling closer to those who are similar to us in wealth, culture, education, and race than to those who are our brothers by baptism into Christ.

What is the point of baptising a child and not incorporating him? Of course he will become God's son—but where will he meet his family? Of course he will get grace, but that grace is to love others, and where will he learn to exercise it?

Christ's will is not to unite us just to himself, but to unite us to each other: 'That they may be one.' Christ is never present in the life of a person who seeks him while excluding others. Everything in us that is purely private, everything proper to us, is condemned to disappear. 'May the body of

Christ keep thy soul to life everlasting.' Only that in us which lives by Christ is saved and made immortal. Only that part of us which is incorporated into Christ will have life everlasting, only what he animates with the same life we share with others. For Christ was *the* man who wanted to save nothing for himself, who kept no part of himself 'private'; the man who becomes just anyone; absolutely anyone can receive and take possession of him.

Giving communion is a terrifying thing to do: to have to entrust Christ to absolutely anyone—children, those whose minds are miles away, the worldly, the neurotic, all these people whose mouths are open but whose hearts cannot be seen. Mentally we compare ourselves with him—with all our fears, our prejudices, our antipathies, our selfishness, our rigidity. We are difficult, critical, dissatisfied—but God makes us his brothers and sisters. 'Though he was in the form of God' (Phil 2:6)—he came from a good family, a good background—Christ 'did not count equality with God a thing to be grasped, but emptied himself, taking the form of a servant, being born in the likeness of men' (vv. 6f.)—any men, ordinary men—'and being found in human form he humbled himself' (v. 8).

Whereas with us, what determines our sympathies and our friendships is not, alas, our baptism, but all kinds of miserable differences: I am rich, he is poor; I come from one kind of family, he from another; I am educated, he is not; I am working-class, he is middle-class. And we forget our fundamental similarity: he is of Christ, and so am I.

The world's benediction to its newborn runs something like this: May he be independent, powerful, rich, at ease. But Christ's wish is: That he may learn to love, to be at the service of others, to be poor, meek, hungry for justice, upright, and merciful—and to make him all these things, he gives him to us in the church. Paradox indeed! We want to save ourselves, and we are put in charge of saving others. We want to cling to God alone, and we are told to be united to our fellows. We want to enter heaven, and here we are, introduced into the society of a mass of all too earthly brethren.

Christ's religion is meant to be lived in a church, in a body—but not to be imprisoned there. Christ took a body not to save it, but to save the world. 'No salvation outside the church' expresses, if we understand it correctly, the missionary vocation of christians, their worldwide responsibility. The church is 'a light for revelation to the Gentiles' (Lk 2 : 32), not a bedside lamp for christians.

We must beware of turning the church into a conservatory for pious souls. Salt is meant to be taken out of the salt-cellar and every mass closes with a sending, a mission that sends the christian assembly out throughout the world. Religious ceremonies should not absorb our energy, but produce it. One can easily relax, and spend one's day in morning prayer, mass, high mass, benediction, vespers and compline, convinced that one is doing very well. But, as I said earlier, we do not live to eat; we eat to live. Prayer must never cease, and therefore it fits in very well with work. The Lord didn't give us the command to 'Come and gaze on me', but to 'Go . . . and make disciples of all nations' (Mt 28:19). When we pray, it should be that 'the Lord of the harvest . . . send out labourers into his harvest' (Mt 9:37). If we pray sincerely, many will be sent.

A 'catholic milieu' is a contradiction in terms. Yet it appears as though the great apostolic ambition of a great many catholic-action leaders is to form solid 'catholic blocs'. A child is placed in a catholic nursery school, a catholic school, a catholic college. As soon as this process is complete, we try to get him into every possible catholic group—whether at work or recreation. Having finally died under the care of a catholic doctor, this salt of the earth will have salted nothing, and this leaven will have been studiously kept apart from the dough. We have created for ourselves a mentality of preservation—preserving our faith, our children, our integrity, our peace of mind. Yet all this energy that we use to 'defend' ourselves ought really to be used for those we are meant to be illuminating. The dimension of catholicism is the universe. The christian community has no bounds narrower than the human race.

To be baptised is necessarily to be a missionary, for it is to be made like to Christ who came not to save himself but others. Baptism doesn't provide us with a reserved place in heaven; it gives us a part to play in evangelising the world. It can only save us by making us into saviours. Anyone who is too anxious to save his soul will lose it. The servant who appears on the last day with only his own talent will be asked, 'Where are the rest?' Yet this talent is intact, pure, well preserved in fact, wrapped carefully in a cloth. All in vain: he is damned. We shall be asked that same question: 'Where are the rest? Show us the others? You by yourself are of no interest to anyone. Hell is the heaven of the solitary.'

I believe in the church . . .

I believe that the church is more than the men who constitute it, more than what unbelievers can see in it. It isn't the whole Christ (the body is not the head), but it belongs to him and lives his life. In the church the cause of salvation is permanently and bodily present in the world: the church is the epiphany of Christ. God can't easily make himself recognised. Christ manifested himself most fully as God by staying on the cross. Yet who would be able to see God in this greater love?

Christ is also bound for ever to the church by love, the church which is as much his cross as his body, and he has made it into a word of God, which astounds and convinces us more than all the miracles of his earthly life. The church is of course not perfect like Christ. The union in it of what is of God and what is of man, isn't 'hypostatic'—it doesn't go so far as to make the person of God who animates it responsible for *everything* it does. But the powers its head gives it possess an extent, a fruitfulness, and a permanence far beyond what he himself did. 'It is to your advantage that I go away' (Jn 16:7); 'Greater works than these will [you] do, because I go to the Father' (Jn 14:12).

One flock and one shepherd was Christ's wish, and that is the mission of his body. It will be fulfilled as long as our own devotion, self-effacement, and docility to the shepherd makes it possible for others to encounter not us, but him.

But there is another sense in which we must believe in the church: the church isn't only the hierarchy, but also—indeed, above all—the faithful. Living by the life of Christ, and given the charge of radiating and even transmitting that life, they also are an object of faith because each one is something greater than just himself. If we can—and indeed must—love our neighbour with the love of God, it is because God who is in himself inaccessible to us has chosen to show himself to us through our humblest brethren.

How is it possible to love a man with the love of God? With a love coming from God and going to God? Only by faith. Without faith, charity hesitates and doubts itself. To have no faith in someone yet 'love them all the same' is an edifying turn of phrase for hating them. You can only really love someone if you do believe in him—in other words, if you see through appearances to his real self. You may know him well—in his family, his circle of friends, his parish, but if you stop there, your love has lost its courage. We must love in everyone the hidden God who can only develop if he is recognised.

For obviously, if God commands us to love others with his own love, it is no merely arbitrary order unconnected with the reality of the situation. Nor is it the result of some kind of mathematical reckoning: 'My friends' friends are my friends. Two things equal to a third thing are equal to each other. I love God . . . God loves others . . . Let us all be friends.' All this is hopelessly beside the point. What kind of love loves to order? If I love others 'for love of God', am I loving them at all? If I love them because I am virtuous, I may well be loving my virtue—but do I love anyone else? It is fatal to make others the occasion, or springboard, for our own merits.

Suppose we go a bit deeper: when we say 'God loves others', what that means is the incarnation and the redemption; it means that he gives himself, communicates himself to them—or that at least he offers himself to them, calls them, draws them with all the force and reality of his love. We are obsessed by the devil's tempting us; but God tempts us far more than the devil, for he is infinitely more powerful and loving than the devil is powerful and hating. We are well aware that the devil is working upon the just, but hesitate to believe that God is working upon the sinful. Many who, night after night piously recite: 'Be sober and watch, for your adversary the devil goeth about like a roaring lion, seeking whom he may devour', feel that the devil will never cease to harass them, and yet really seem to believe that God abandons those who persist in sin.

From the moment of the incarnation, Christ became one with all men. He is 'the true light that enlightens every man ... coming into the world' (Jn 1:9). Christ exerts a real influence in every human being, calling him so that his whole fate is changed whatever his answer to the call; there is a point at which his nature can lay hold of its redemption, at which God's love breaks into him, at least as a 'temptation'.

And which of us can boast that we have totally rejected him? (Only Mary ever consented totally, and fortunately there doesn't exist any antithesis to her in the order of damnation!) No one totally escapes God. No one is vigilant enough, clear-sighted enough, wicked enough, to recognise and reject him under every guise in which he presents himself to us. You may say 'no' to him as a priest, or as the church, or as morality, or as christian political theory—it is easy enough to reject him in all these guises. But if you love the poor, or hate injustice, if you respond to the innocence, purity, freshness of childhood, if you enjoy the beauties of nature, if you ever know feelings of affection, of pity, of wonder—then whatever your explicit faith you are saying 'yes' to God in all these guises. I do not say that you are necessarily in a state of grace, but simply that you are being infiltrated by graces, that you are threatened, encircled, invaded by the vast, patient, humble love of God: 'Behold, I stand at the door and knock' (Rev 3:20).

We believe in a God who raises the dead. The history of the church, and of each one of us, is a succession of deaths and resurrections—of resurrections coming at the very moment when we are tempted to resign ourselves to death. To be in the church means to have faith in the continual death and resurrection of Christ, God made man. We must believe in that death and resurrection in others, in the church, and in ourselves. If the church were obvious, satisfactory, uncontrovertible, it would be merely human. It is because the church demands our faith that it is divine. If you are satisfied by its appearances, then you should leave the church at once; you should not be in the church if being there involves you in no suffering. The church should force you to go beyond appearances and keep re-living, for yourself and others, the mystery of death and resurrection entrusted to it. At every moment it must cast off its outworn forms, its compromises, its sins, and constantly bathe in the waters of purification to rise new and pure, without spot or wrinkle, holy and immaculate before God.

There is only one unforgivable sin, one final condemnation: that is to be an old man, a man who wants to stay old, who holds back the redemption of the world, and blocks the world's resurrection by lack of faith. To look backwards, to delay, to be a conservative (of the dead!), to trust only what one sees, to lack faith in the constant youth and renewal of the church and of the world—that is the 'old man' castigated by St Paul. It is our job to collaborate with all our faith in the building up of the body of Christ which, being 'joined and knit together by every joint with which it is supplied, when each part is working properly,

makes bodily growth and upbuilds itself in love'
(Eph 4:16).

One need only look at the church now, to see it
breaking out, seeding, flowering at every point
when it was thought dying or dead. What new
shoots, what providential coincidences, what
wonderful encounters are now bearing witness
that it is the same Spirit at work giving rise to the
same aspirations and fulfilments at every point of
christianity. Biblical studies, liturgy, theology—all
are newly alive; marriage, the community, lay
spirituality, the realities of this world—our understanding of all these things has suddenly deep-
ened. Everywhere there are astounding outpour-
ings of the Spirit.

It is our faith in the church, and in husband
or wife, in children or parents, in community or
parish, that will make them rise from the dead,
and make of them all a real church.

11
The communion
of saints

The phrase 'communion of saints' really has two meanings: a communion in holy things, and a communion among saints (remembering that this latter means not virtuous people, but has St Paul's sense of all who belong to the church, the people of God).

In the first meaning we are saying: I believe that God communicates himself to us through visible things. The reign of the Holy Ghost is not an 'invisible' way of life. In it sensible things are filled with supernatural meaning and power, and bring us into direct contact with the presence of the Holy Spirit. His means of communication are chosen from the simplest things—water, oil, bread, a priest! Matter is in no sense excluded from redemption—one day it will be wholly saved, and even now it aspires and works towards that renewal. All those creatures that will one day be associated in our everlasting happiness already collaborate in our present salvation. Everything is redeemed. It is not a question of being saved by the skin of our teeth, but of being saved lock, stock, and barrel. Everything we love—animals, flowers, trees, sky, and water, all 'creation waits with eager longing for the revealing of the sons of God . . . because the creation itself will be set free from its bondage to decay and obtain the glorious liberty of the children of God' (Rom 8:19, 21). The incarnation goes beyond mankind; it extends to the whole world, and makes use of the whole world to win men. Bread is obedient to a word that makes it become the body of Christ; at a word the wine lets itself become his blood. If we could only imitate them! When will God be able to say but the word, and *our* soul will be healed?

Earth is the sacrament of heaven. Everything we can seen is an announcement and a preparation for what we cannot see. The seed rotting in the earth so as to spring into fresh life is an elementary form of the sacrament of baptism, in which we die to rise to a wider life. And baptism itself is but the sign of the death and resurrection of Christ, of the only life by which we shall live forever.

From the very first, the incarnation called for faith to discern the divine so mingled with the human. Once God was no longer in his heaven, it was harder to adore him. Once God leaves our imagination and enters our neighbourhood, it is something of a shock. 'This is a hard saying; who can listen to it?' (Jn 6:60) said the disciples when Christ had told them of the bread of life, his perpetual incarnation. The sacraments involve the most earthly elements in the most divine action. All creation is both the means and the object of salvation.

But generally, we understand the communion of saints in its second sense: a communion of persons, an exchange of influence among the blessed in heaven, the faithful on earth, and the souls in purgatory. What does this mean? A single life circulates among all those who are incorporated into Christ. Jesus was born, lived, suffered and died for others. All who are united to him are united with one another: they do not live, or suffer, or die alone. Because we belong to his body, because we live by his life, because we are the one Christ, we can pray for one another, make promises for one another, and be, in a certain sense, answerable for one another.

We believe this union to be so close as to be infinitely beyond any blood-relationship; it makes us closer than brother and sister, than parent and child. 'Who is my mother', asked Christ, 'and who are my brothers?' (Mt 12:48). Because we are in God's image, to be in the church is to be 'one as they are one'.

Every christian is, in a sense, within all the others; we are invisibly bound to all mankind. To penetrate the hearts of those we love, we have at our disposal a far subtler weapon than our own feeble words and actions. We are no longer hampered by distance, nor by the more cruel disability of our own clumsiness and insensitivity. There is a point at which we are all brought together and at which we can communicate. There is a way open to us to do all the good that is bursting within us which must otherwise either be repressed or explode uselessly. We can ease, help, comfort, and cheer people with whom we have no contact. 'That they may be one' was Christ's wish: that one life may circulate among them, that there may be a contact and solidarity among all these living stones in the same building, these branches of the same vine, these members of the same body. We receive life only in order to hand it on. To stop communicating it is to stop the life flowing, to compromise the life of the whole body. But, on the other hand, as long as these dead members remain in the body, they can still be helped by the living ones whose very vitality enables them to revitalise the areas where death has set in. What is paralysed can always be brought back into action by what is alive.

Salvation is not an individual affair. Either we rise together with all the innumerable beings for whom we are answerable to God—or we are involved in their damnation; we shall not enter heaven alone. All of us can, I think, be judged simply by pointing to the scope of our interests. For some, it is identical with what one may call their own circumference. These are the damned. Others extend their attention to those around them. But can we really be called 'catholics' if our vision does not reach to the ends of the earth, and the boundaries of time? If you can be resigned to the damnation of a single creature, then you aren't a christian. If we had prayed and loved enough, there would be no damned. Until the last saint has said his last prayer, we cannot be certain that the whole world is not saved.

This 'collectivism' of salvation is an alarming thought to the many christians who think of their baptism as having given them, individually, a right to heaven. And others would protest against it on the grounds of their 'personality'. This mystical body seems to them an anonymous crowd, a faceless mass, a lumping together, a kind of heavenly jam in which we are saved by losing all identity.

The world of today is looking for ways to bring people together, while still respecting their individuality. Nazism and communism can be seen in this light as two misdirected attempts at uniting a still half-blind humanity. Two thousand years ago Christ died to unite in a single body the scattered children of God. Only the power of the risen Christ's love is enough to gather together all men while letting them all develop freely. 'That they may be one as we are one.' The world tries to become one, but not as the Father and Son are one, alas. With nazism the unity sought was a unity through blood, a racial unity. With communism, it is work which is to achieve the goal, satisfying all man's needs.

We are being unceasingly spurred on by the Holy Ghost to love others a bit more, to be a little more disturbed at the sufferings of others, a little happier over their joys. The more we enter into this solidarity with others, the more alive, the more enlightened, the more aware we shall ourselves become—until the moment comes when we form that one body, where God is all in all. We have the promise of eternal life. We know the meaning of history. We know the explanation of what is happening. That is why we must proclaim our message to the world which is hungry for it, and which is already groping for it in the darkness. Racism, communism; what other lamentable solution will it try in its great longing for unity? If only, instead of our usual pathetic end-of-the-world-prize-giving, we could preach to the world this magnificent building up of the body of Christ, with all the members more alive by being more firmly united, and more firmly united by being more alive!

We are also in communion with the dead; yet our attitude to them is generally quite incompatible with real faith in the communion of saints. Even the best christians are surprised to find when they think about it how little they believe in anything but physical presence, human agency, the world they can see and touch. Death seems such a break, such a painful loss, that the words of faith seem meaningless, the formulae of christianity so false that we dare not utter them. We shut ourselves up in our grief; we even think that our faithfulness to the departed is best expressed by despair. Nothing could be more untrue, for sorrow is generally quite selfish. Some people think of it as ennobling, as elevating, as a way of making good past failures, but the opposite is the case. It turns us in upon ourselves, shrivels us up, closes us to others. When we lose those we love, we grieve, but only because we have no longer got them, because we can no longer have the joy of their presence and their love. That was the selfishness Jesus deprecated when he said:

But now I am going to him who sent me; yet none of you asks me, 'Where are you going?' But because I have said these things to you, sorrow has filled your hearts. [Jn 16:5f.]

If we were generous and believing, if we really cared for them and not only for ourselves, we should wonder where they were going—we should be so interested in their fate that we should want to follow them in thought wherever they went and, knowing that their sufferings were at an end and that they were with the Father, we shouldn't be able to do other than rejoice with them. 'If you loved me, you would have rejoiced', said our Lord, 'because I go to the Father' (Jn 14:28). Yet how many christians fail to ask, 'Where are you going?' If we really do so, we must go with them in mind into this infinitely superior and happier state; rather than turning in upon ourselves in solitude, we should rejoice in their joy.

Yet how rarely we do so. There is a pagan sorrow in far too many christian funerals, a sense of despair in having lost someone, of finality in bidding him farewell. We feel we have lost him forever, and must shut him out of our hearts. The way we give him up for lost because we think we are cut off from him, the way we try to cure ourselves of thinking about him and expunge him from our life, is like killing him over again. For a real believer, however, the dead person becomes more alive than before, with a life that makes him closer to us in a new kind of way. When he was on earth, there were a thousand barriers between us. Now at last, he has become completely available, attentive, free to give us all the love and care we need. If he needs prayers, then he depends upon us as never before—and we depend on him and his intercession far more, too. The burial mass should be the beginning of this new sense of his presence, just as it is our daily initiation into the real presence, and the nourishing and strengthening action upon us of another who died a tragic death, yet whom we believe to be far more alive than we are.

There can be no loneliness in the communion of saints. The christian does more than merely piously preserve the memory of the dead. He prays to them, consults them, takes inspiration from them, keeps returning to them; as a result he becomes open to that spiritual world which it is so hard to believe in unless one is introduced to it by those one has loved best. Indeed, perhaps the greatest service we can do to those we love, is to draw them with us when we leave this world for the next. That is one sense in which we can understand our Lord's saying, 'It is to your advantage that I go away' (Jn 16 : 7).

The early christians used to call the day of death *dies natalis*—birthday, the day when life begins. For on that day the life of the dead man becomes more alive, more effective, more active, happier, and the life of those left behind whose faith in the world of the spirit receives new life from communicating with their dead. These sad dates should be feasted as birthdays.

That is what happened at Christ's resurrection. His death was his birthday, his resurrection into true life, and it was from that moment that the apostles began finding him always with them. They possessed him within them far better than when he was among them. They heard him, they consulted him, they felt the life he constantly communicated to them springing up within them and giving them inspiration. Like a father who dies when his children are too young to take in all he wants to tell them, Jesus had said to them:

> I have yet many things to say to you, but you cannot bear them now. When the Spirit of truth comes, he will guide you into all truth. [Jn 16: 12f.]

The apostles felt the life and inspiration of that Spirit gradually mounting within them.

Many people think that all this is too lofty for them; hard sayings, and who shall bear them? And yet we really know that this is how it must be, and that only thus can God be as good, as alive, as just as he must be—that anything else would be unworthy of God. Since our Lord died, his presence is truer and more complete, his Spirit is everywhere. Now bread truly nourishes us, and even a fragment gives life and strength for ever. Now wine really makes us joyful, and a few drops in a chalice will exalt and delight us for ever. Water really washes, oil anoints, the human word binds and looses—all is filled, penetrated with the

Spirit, and all who feel his touch know from experience the truth of the words:

It is to your advantage that I go away, for if I do not go away, the Counsellor will not come to you. [Jn 16:7.]

If you loved me, you would have rejoiced, because I go to the Father. [Jn 14:28.]

12
The forgiveness of sins

This is not the cliché we are inclined to think!

A great many people make their own private abridgement of the creed; they believe only in sin. Being pessimistic and conservative, they believe firmly in the power, the permanence, and the rule, of sin. They are sure 'the world won't change'. To them it is a waste of time dreaming of utopias, of social progress, of improving education, of personal development, of international unity, of any solidarity with the under-developed nations. Original sin is there. You cannot get away from it.

They follow this profession of faith with a few tears for our sad and sinful state, and continue cheerfully to take advantage of the things sin does for them. They draw their dividends, and go to mass every Sunday. But original sin is wiped out by baptism. It is an over-simplification to make it the explanation and excuse for everything that goes wrong in the world. The world goes wrong because we, though redeemed, sanctified, and adopted by the Father, start to sin all over again every day, just as Adam did. We commit sins we needn't commit, sins for which we are totally responsible; and we should commit fewer if we did not so readily blame them onto Adam. God has 'most wonderfully renewed' human nature: the redemption has placed us in a state superior to Adam's. It hasn't, of course, abolished sin. Another misconstruction of the creed is to believe in 'exemption from sin' in paradise as something already present, in a world with no more disputes, lies, or betrayals.

The truth lies between these two extremes: the redemption takes effect in humility—not through exemption from sin, but through forgiveness. It is in this that our condition is superior to Adam's. We are in an order that is irrevocable. Adam had only to sin once, and he lost God's gifts forever. But for us, grace never stops flowing. Forgiveness is always to be had. We are bound to God in an 'eternal covenant', a marriage where there is no divorce. God has espoused us, and however unworthy, however unfaithful we are to him, he will never cast us off. Since he loves us for no merit of our own, our faults never discourage him from loving and forgiving us.

The good news of the gospel is bad news to many, bringing a terrible disillusionment: Go, and preach the forgiveness of sins! They thought they were just, but they find they are sinners! They thought their efforts were pleasing to God, but they find that the way to please him best is to be forgiven. They wanted to honour God by converting others, but who thinks it good news to be told he can now confess his own sins? We should have preferred—receiving the redemption with a renewal of the original sin of pride, self-sufficiency, and autonomy which its purpose was to repair— not to have to sin any more, to have no more need of forgiveness.

But if you love God (and not just yourself), you must share his joy in the remission of sins. You will not greet it with the displeasure that betrays selfishness. Nowhere can we come closer to God than in the place of forgiveness. We shall not go to heaven because we are pleased with ourselves. We shall be saved because we are pleased with God, delighted with God, overjoyed by the goodness and generosity of God. What we shall proclaim in heaven are not our own victories and merits, but the lovingkindness of God's pardon.

No child realises how much his mother loves him until he is ill. She loves him always, of course, but dares not really show it fully, for fear that she might spoil him. But when he is in pain, then she can have the joy of pouring out all the love she normally keeps bottled up. That is why malicious wits say that man's illnesses are his wife's delight. Not only because, at that moment, she takes over and becomes mistress of the situation, but because at last she can show him how she loves him. Normally, he has always gone before she has had time to tell him (for the feminine tactic of wanting him to guess at it takes time). She feels helpless, because he doesn't seem to need her. But when he is there, tied to his bed by illness, he is at her

6—c.

mercy, and she can love and care for him to her heart's content.

God is the same. It is when we are ill, when at last we realise our sickness, as sinners, helplessly drawn to evil and to death, that God can tell us his love, his joy in taking us in, looking after us, healing us. When we are healthy, we run so fast that he cannot catch hold of us. But when at last we sink down in the confessional, God at last has time and opportunity to explain how much he loves us—unless we are in too much of a hurry to snatch up our receipt and go.

It is important to stress this at the end of a retreat. All too often we depart with a sense of exaltation—we shall change everything, we shall exercise perfect charity from now on. Inevitably depression results, for what is blown up must in the end become flat again. The christian attitude is to say: we shall try and we shall often fail. Every day we shall stumble; we have fallen too often in the past not to realise that. But God will forgive us every time, and we shall be able to forgive one another because he will be with us to help. We shall not suddenly be able to persevere without fail, but we shall always be able to begin again, humbly. We cannot promise never to quarrel, but we can beg each other's pardon. And if we have the Holy Spirit even a little within us, our reconciliations will be deeper than our previous understanding. All our hope must lie in making use of God's unceasing offer of forgiveness. Our delight, then, must be to make better and more frequent confessions!

The christian message has always been a call to repentance—not to a miserable, masochistic chewing over our sins, but to a turning to God in the hope of forgiveness. John the Baptist 'went into all the region about the Jordan, preaching a baptism of repentance for the forgiveness of sins' (Lk 3:3).

Now after John was arrested, Jesus came into Galilee, preaching the gospel of God, and saying, 'The time is fulfilled, and the kingdom of God is at hand; repent, and believe in the gospel.' [Mk 1:14f.]

And in Acts we see Peter just after Pentecost astounding the crowds with a speech wholly inspired by the Holy Spirit whom he had just received:

Now when they heard this they were cut to the heart, and said to Peter and the rest of the apostles, 'Brethren, what shall we do?' And Peter said to them, 'Repent . . .' [Acts 2:37f.]

The christian message, even since then, has always met with two sorts of response. *Either*

We have Abraham as our father. [Lk 3:8.]

That is, we are irreproachable—virtue is our inheritance, and we can look down upon others from the height of our own genealogical tree. *Or*

The multitudes asked him, 'What shall we do?' And he answered them, 'He who has two coats, let him share with him who has none; and he who has food, let him do likewise.' Tax collectors also came . . . and said to him, 'Teacher, what shall we do?' [Lk 3 : 10–12.]

The same two responses occur today. But the modern pharisees tend to have brightened up their appearance à la Gide. Their justification now takes the form of declaring that they do not attempt to justify themselves: 'Oh yes, I am bitter, envious, lazy, lustful, undependable . . . but at least I don't pretend to be anything else. I'm not hypocritical about it. I thank thee Lord, for having given me the cult of sincerity, and not letting me be like the people who are always acting a part, who don't dare be themselves, who want to climb the social ladder as much as I do, who want to look better than they are, and enjoy life, but give it all up to become little saints in their niches —in what they call their "communities". And what a mess they make of it Lord, just look at them!' They make a mess of it all right. They are the only ones who do make a mess of things. The pharisees of the old kind have a code, duties they carry out; their accounts are invariably up to date, their obligations clear, their repentances ready on the right day, their fastings, their sackcloth, their ashes . . . All this can easily be kept in order given a little willpower and good organisation. The Gide-type pharisees cannot by definition make a mess of things. They make their position quite clear. They are at peace with themselves which is the ultimate success. The more they sin, the more comfort they can take in being different from the 'hypocrites' who cannot understand them because they are too sincere.

But the third kind of person is a poor wretch who is dedicated to fail every day; he wants both to recognise his sin, and never to give up struggling against it. And since he alone has discovered that the New Testament consists not in a defined code, but in an infinite love, and that Christ's commandment is simply to love as God loves—he knows that he has no possible chance of success. His accounts will never be in order.

'I give tithes, I fast twice a week . . . I am not like other men, extortioners, unjust . . .' It is much easier to be self-satisfied along these lines than to admit that our only duty is to love one another. The unfortunates who do so can only use the prayer of the publican: 'Lord have mercy upon me a sinner'. For all those who suffer, who have no faith, who hunger and thirst—for bread and other things—I should have done more.

'Simon, son of John, do you love me?' (Jn 21: 16). That was all Christ asked of Peter before entrusting his church to him. And the mission he went on to give him was the same: Love others, look after others, 'feed my sheep' (v. 17). It is upon love that we shall be judged. But this is far from being a reassuring idea, for love is the one thing that we are quite certain to do badly. A 'supple' morality, said Péguy, is infinitely more demanding than a rigid one. What touches us at every point so that we can never escape it? The rigid metal of armour, or the soft cloth of a perfectly fitting robe?

Sin is not disobeying the third, the sixth, the ninth, or the tenth commandment. Sin consists in not wanting to love the giver of the commandments.

I have come to understand the true nature of penance more clearly as a result of discussions with protestants. 'You catholics', I have been told, 'are dispensed from loving God. You only need imperfect contrition (sorrow motivated by self-interest) to obtain absolution which sets you to rights. We protestants don't believe we are "set to rights" with God unless we have begun to love him again. Your sacrament justifies you in remaining in an inferior state religiously. You pay only the cheapest price for your forgiveness'.

The answer is simple, of course: the sacrament gives us back sanctifying grace, which is precisely the power to love God. Absolution itself leads us back from attrition to contrition. St Thomas even goes so far as to say we must make an act of perfect love as soon as possible after confession. Yet some catholics boast to protestants of the sense of security the sacrament gives them: 'It is hard for you to know whether you feel true sorrow, whether you have really made an act of perfect contrition or not. You are wide open to illusion, to the temptation of finding human means towards that security which we get from the objectivity of the sacrament. We are certain of God's forgiveness because the church declares it to us.'

'But', they reply, 'we don't need human confirmation. God is superior to men. We have infinitely more confidence in his mercy when we seek it than you can possibly have in the mediation of your church.' And they are right—if they separate Christ from his church.

Surely the real explanation should run thus: You ask God 'directly' for forgiveness, God who is in heaven. But for us, God is upon earth—he is with us all days, even to the consummation of the world. He gives himself to us in every one of our brethren. It is not enough to address ourselves to him in heaven; we must ask his pardon in the person of those in whom we have offended him. 'I am Jesus, whom you are persecuting' (Acts 9:5). 'As you did it to one of the least of these my brethren, you did it to me' (Mt 25:40). In other words: 'You have wounded me in my members. You have lacerated my body. That is where you must ask pardon, make good, come back to have your sins forgiven.'

The confessor is simply the representative of the church, in other words of those who have been sinned against and who are kind, patient, ready to forgive. He is the community's witness. But that community must be a reality. When we say the church is 'holy', we mean that she is made up of people who have some element of holiness in them, people who are capable of forgiving, being reconciled, renewing friendly relations with those who have offended us. I often wonder into what community I am reincorporating those who confess their sins to me! It seems to me so clear that the average man is quite incapable of examining his conscience, of repenting, and above all of starting afresh in the solitude he is consigned to. He needs all his brethren—not merely to point out his faults (in which he readily finds help!), but to help him regret them, and want to return, to support him in his efforts to keep faith. All our brethren should be there, with us, at every confession. We might find it a bit disconcerting at first, not being used to it—but what a lot we should gain in sincerity, in enthusiasm, in sense of reality!

What use is it to be reincorporated in solitude? We shut ourselves tightly into a cupboard—in order to declare that we want to become part of a society again. We take care that no one sees or hears us, and declare that we are anxious to enter once more into communion with our brethren. At least when we say the Confiteor we are logical—perhaps because we do not think of what we are saying. There we summon everyone—the saints in heaven and our brothers on earth. We confess before them all and ask them all to forgive us; we beg them to help us to return to grace with God and with them. We admit our guilt: 'through my fault, through my own fault, through my own most grievous fault'. It isn't like confession, where we are inclined to say: 'Father, I don't know how it came about. Such a thing never happened to me before. But really I was at the end of my tether. You have no idea of how aggravating he can be!' No, confession is not the settling of an individual account. It is being restored into the community of our brethren. Each one of us is needed in the church: if we have become a cell outside the life-stream of the body, a dead weight, a dried-up twig, a paralysed and paralysing member, then the grace of God and the love of those around us come to knock on our closed doors begging us to change, to come back to life, to communication, to contact. And now, won over by this loving influence, we have come to say: 'Yes, I should like to come back, I should like to be a living cell once again in the body, to take up my place and my work once more, to be back with my brothers.'

That is what penance really means.

We say, fearfully: 'I should like to be reunited with God.' And we are told, 'Unite yourself with your brothers. I absolve thee of thy sins'. What sins? 'The sins you have committed against God and your brothers.' You are suddenly relieved of your helplessness, set free of your paralysis. God, who brings the dead to life, makes you alive once more, a living cell in a living body. The love of God fills you and thrusts you out towards others.

Penance is a transport of joy, but a 'public transport'. We are transported together with the community of our brothers, and borne along and upheld by them. It is they who make us pass from death to life: 'We know that we have passed out of death into life, because we love the brethren' (1 Jn 3 : 14).

Penance re-establishes us in communion with Christ's eucharistic body, but also—and far more important—with his mystical body. 'Go to confession before going to communion' used to be the rule. But we were never told that confession is a form of communion. We should emerge from the confessional to go eagerly to our brothers. They are waiting for us (or they should be) to receive us back into their fraternity. The love of our brothers looks after us and heals us from the miseries of sin. We aren't merely absolved, but fêted and loved.

The love and forgiveness of men are a sacrament of the love and forgiveness of God.

13
The resurrection of the body and life everlasting

Bringing these two articles of the creed together into a single proposition of itself helps us to understand them a little better, for it gets us out of the rut in which the hopes of a great many christians are bogged down. They don't really believe in the resurrection of the body, and therefore have no very ardent longing for life everlasting. They imagine a heaven full of souls, with cherubim and seraphim, dominations and powers—a totally disembodied life except for a rather old-fashioned decor of palms, thrones, and crowns; and the whole time to be spent in contemplating (without a break or let-up) the majesty of God. Even if you add music to the picture it is hardly irresistible!

Who will describe for us the kind of heaven we should want to go to? The resurrection of the body is the restoration of the whole man, with all his human dreams and joys, all his human affections. Christ opens up for us a life of everlasting happiness, and the resurrection of the body makes it clear that this supernatural happiness will also be a human happiness.

We must never think of the effect of the redemption as meaning simply that our corpse will come alive again. The word *body* (or *flesh*) here means the whole of man, with the weakness of his nature, as opposed to the life-giving energy of the Spirit of God. When we say, 'The Word became flesh', we don't mean that God took a human body, but that he became a man. And when the bible says that 'man is but flesh', it doesn't mean that man is nothing but meat! Christ isn't talking of the immortality of the soul, but of the resurrection of man—either for punishment, or for a life of happiness.

Heaven will be very much to our liking—as long as we have good taste, that is! Obviously, if it is to be divinised, everything in us must be purified and transformed; but far from this turning us into angels, it will make us more human. To become detached from affection, from joy, and from pleasure is not the only way of getting to heaven. A deep and faithful attachment can also take us there. The christian ideal is not to wait patiently for the end of this sinful world, but to anticipate it, to work to bring about the first beginnings of the kingdom of God. There will be continuity and discontinuity. Heaven will not be a straightforward continuation of this world. Though a heaven full of souls is not a particularly attractive prospect, neither is a heaven that merely eternalises life as it is now. We may one day find

a way to prolong the lives of old people in-
definitely, but it is not at all certain that this will
increase the pleasures of life, either for themselves
or anyone else.

There is a value in asking each one of us: Who
wants to live for ever? Who finds life so good as
to want it never to end? Is there anything in your
life that you would like to last for *ever*? Is there
anyone you love enough to want them to be there
for *ever*? Anyone for whose sake you would like
to live for ever yourself? Do you love the created
world enough to want it to share your eternity?
Or have you carefully excluded it in order to save
your own soul? The death of Bernanos' country
priest is especially fine for the redemptive love it
reveals: 'I have loved men greatly, and this land
of the living has been very dear to me. I shall not
die without weeping . . .' Those who die like that
will take with them into the kingdom the part of
this world they have loved so well as to discover
its loveliness. We shall be saved with everything
we have loved. Our hope of redemption is in proportion to our capacity for love.

Who really wants an eternal world, an everlasting life? It would be a crushing burden. Only God
could bear an eternity of living; only God loves
enough to make the idea of going on for ever anything but terrifying. When Christ promises us life
everlasting, it is a participation in *his* life. It does
not mean the immortality of the soul, or life in
this world all over again: it is a life of love. Christ
is the resurrection and the life because he offers us
a share in a life so rich and rewarding that we

cannot want, or even imagine, its ending. To be weary of life means that one is not living his life, that one is not loving (which we tend to express in the terms: 'No one loves me'). To long for life to end means that one is not yet worthy to have it fulfilled. At fifteen one can face the idea of dying with equanimity, and is astonished and somewhat scornful at the prudence of adults, with their fears and their clinging to life. But not yet to have tasted and appreciated life means that one must not die yet awhile. This is not the moment to make life eternal.

Our life will be made perfect only when we want it to go on for ever. We must not die before then! Present life, future life, and eternal life. We mustn't imagine heaven as a continuation of this world, nor as a completely new world. The temptation, of course, is to look forward to a reversal: the greater one's disappointments in this valley of tears, the greater one's merits and thus one's future happiness. And equally, every joy in this world must be paid for by a proportionate punishment in the next (for pleasure marks you out automatically for damnation). You must suffer, and the only choice you have is whether to do so now or later. This theory of compensation is a most popular over-simplification.

Eternal life began for us with baptism. We are in eternity. Those who have received no joy from the presence and love of God in this world won't know him in the next. The whole purpose of our trial in this world is to make us accustomed to God and give us a taste for his blessedness. We do nothing in this world except meet God under all the signs and appearances through which he wants to teach and call us, and find out whether we should enjoy being with him for ever. If we have not learnt to love him, then there is no point in going to heaven; we should wander endlessly and uneasily around, seeking our favourite sins, and unable to find anything attractive in what delights everyone else—as out of place as a cow in church.

The kingdom of God is within us, now. If there are times when we do not feel this foretaste a joy and illumination, then we should be deeply concerned, for we are in danger of never really knowing it. The gifts of the Holy Spirit ought to make us able to experience the things of God; if those things mean nothing to us, it is because we are resisting him. He enables us *recta sapere*—to taste and enjoy right things. Without him we will find them as insipid in heaven as we do on earth. The only eternal life we shall have is that which has already begun.

I think that hell may well be the continuation of the pleasures we have sought here: an uninterrupted fashionable party; innumerable loveless contacts; an empty agitation and feverishness. There will be no need of furnaces or pitchforks or boiling oil to torment anyone. There will just be small 'gas stoves': pleasures forced to continue for ever—how infinitely preferable it would be to work! All the damned will have are the things they sought so eagerly on earth: success, amusements, money, freedom—things whose hellish nature they often sensed, but to which they still returned with perverse obstinacy. They won't be cast out, suppressed, or tortured, but only made eternal as they are. All they asked was to be left in peace? Alas, they will be left in peace for ever. The branch cut off from the vine withers away; every time we experience a sense of withering, of drying out, of shrivelling up, we are experiencing something of hell. Hell is never-ending disintegration. It begins on earth with inward anarchy, hardness, isolation. It becomes complete in solitude, chaos, the erosion of human potential, the terrible liberty of being held by no ties of any kind, no love at all.

Hell and heaven are within us. If you know anything at all about human nature, you know how one can nourish and cherish and with perfect lucidity prefer one's hell. Man is not only capable of damning himself, but actually wants to do so. He can love evil because he does evil and is evil. Which of us hasn't, even as a child, been so consumed with rage as to prefer to destroy everything rather than mend things, to die and see everyone else die rather than forgive or ask forgiveness. Which of us hasn't experienced those urges to despair when one has hugged one's miseries to oneself instead of accepting comfort from those one loves and becoming happy and good once more?

Heaven will also be a new birth to the best we have known on earth. Have I loved God's pardon? Then he will pardon me for ever. Have I believed? Now I shall see. Have I delighted in his works? There will be more to marvel at every day.

Have I noted and studied the structures of things? I will learn ever more about what fascinates me, and with God as guide will discover all the truth I have patiently and reverently sought here. Have I had a sense of joy and resurrection after communion with God and my fellow men? I shall remain always with those I love. Have I known joy from poverty, from compassion, from fighting for justice and true peace, from being persecuted, from mercy? Then I have already entered beatitude; to enjoy all these things is to enjoy God. We must not dream of some future life that will make up to us for our present sad one, and dispense us from trying to improve matters. We must begin now to live a life that can last for ever.

The central question today, which ought to unite christian and atheist, but in fact divides them, is this: How do you imagine the end of the world? Do you think God will come down from above at the end of time, and bring us a prefabricated paradise, or do you think he will invite us to construct it with his help? Will the end of the world be a disaster or a completion? Will God put an end to our pains when he thinks we have put up with them long enough, or will the world only end when it is complete? Will human effort play a part in God's plan, or will it be looked upon as something that merely kept us 'happy and busy'?

Now at last, in the twentieth century, we are beginning to achieve the means and realise the need to feed the undernourished two-thirds of the human race—to give them that minimum of comfort that makes it possible to profit from the redemption. For the first time in history, a collective, worldwide conscience is being born and felt in humanity. Despite all the defences of selfishness and the fears of conservatism, a growing equality in social conditions, and a greater awareness of solidarity among both individuals and peoples, are making our contemporaries more and more ready to fulfil Christ's great prayer 'that they all may be one'.

This whole great movement of liberation follows the same direction as our effort at redemption. The conversion of the world is unthinkable without an economic, social, and technological transformation of the kind that is now taking place. As Père Malevez says: 'Present-day control over matter, political organisation, art, thought, and technology are bringing Christ to completion, and thus to glory.... Catholicism welcomes human progress in all these directions as a condition, and indeed a component, of its own perfection' (*Nouvelle Revue Théologique*, 1937, 377). Christians should therefore be vying in zeal and generosity with the most eager supporters of this evolution. The great obstacles today to the real humanisation of our planet are now moral ones: selfishness, fear, and pride. It is our job as christians to proclaim and prove that they can be surmounted.

Yet alas, with humanity on the threshold of an astounding movement forward, christians hold aside, and predict every kind of disaster. In a way they are right, for the higher one goes, the greater one's risk of falling, but Cassandra is surely a lamentable role for the heralds of the good news of redemption to be playing. We are certainly right to fear that our contemporaries may fall a prey to pride, making progress an end in itself, without God and indeed against God. The danger is a real one. But it is exaggerated by pessimistic theologians and unenlightened believers who can see no place or interest in christianity for this progress, evident and exciting though it is; and who think that to be a christian one must become divided, torn between the world and God, with no possible way of bringing the two together. Yet it is excellent theology to believe in precisely that: the universal dominion of Christ, his cosmic pleroma.

I sometimes wonder whether christians are not assisting—though unconsciously, since they have so weakened, idealised, and individualised it—at the beginning of the fulfilment of their hopes. It would be terrible for us to wait to take part in it until the moment of victory won by others. In vain should we claim that these truths had always been in the 'deposit' of revelation. We should have preserved them with so little care, and they have rediscovered them with so much courage and satisfaction, that *we* might not even be able to recognise them in the picture of light and youth they show us, and *they* would refuse to recognise them in the picture we pull out from beneath layers of dust. Indeed, this situation already exists: our contemporaries are seeking a faith, a sect, a myth, a salvation. But they are determined not to apply to the 'professionals'. The leaven has lost touch with—and lost the confidence of—the lump. The official circles of religion are so riddled with empty forms and shells, so void of life.

The matter can be summed up thus: Does Christ leave us in the world to prove our good will by 'using this world as though we used it not' until he frees us by bringing us—paternalistically —into a heaven that will replace the world which will have been destroyed? Or has he filled the world with natural and supernatural forces that can gradually transform it, making it a place of justice where men love one another?

But surely, one may say, revelation, the gospel, the epistles all speak of a violent ending, a destruction of the world? Yes, but other texts suggest the opposite: they speak not of annihilation, but of regeneration and restoration; they speak of the end coming unexpectedly, coming as a surprise (cf. Mt 24:37). These texts are not contradictory. The same is true of them as of those which refer to the number of the elect, or the hour of the parousia. They appear to be saying different things, but thereby leave an uncertainty which is precisely the scope for our action, the occasion for our initiative, the measure of our freedom.

Were they more precise we should be discouraged from acting—either through despair or excessive security. It is as paralysing to initiative to be told that all are saved as to know that any given person is damned. In either case we can have no part to play; our collaboration is not needed. Similarly, whether the end of the world will be tomorrow, or in twenty million years, to know the date would be paralysing. If we are uncertain, then we can work to hasten it (2 Pet 3:12), we have a measure of responsibility. Christ's coming depends on us. Equally, whether the parousia is a disaster or a fulfilment hangs upon our efforts and our understanding—and these are stimulated by that very uncertainty. Everything suggests that we need to be left a clear field, to have an awareness of our responsibility, by seeing the two possible ends—one dreadful, the other glorious—to which our choice can lead.

Further, it may be that this fruitful alternative is merely two ways of looking at the same event. The Book of Revelation is the revelation of what is hidden. Thus the harvest is the apocalypse of the grain of wheat. It is a festival first and foremost, even if it is also a cutting down. Birth is the revelation of a baby. But the pains of childbirth are forgotten in joy that a man is born into the world. And those pains are certainly not something in the future—we are undergoing them now. It is clear that a new world is coming to birth. Many of the events that seem to us ultimate and solemn may in fact be realities of every day.

The 'end of the world' has already taken place: at Christ's death, the earth shook, the sun was darkened, the dead rose, the Prince of this world was cast out, and those who saw it were seized with fear and cried, 'Truly this was the Son of God' (Mt 27:54). But it has been suspended, so that vast numbers of men can take advantage of it. The capital eschatological event consists in the death and resurrection of Christ. Modern exegetes stress the fact that it is essentially complete: 'The judgement of God has been revealed, victory is won, the final option set forth, and the words spoken which will not pass away when heaven and earth do.' But the manifestation of Christ's glory and the completion of the kingdom remain to be accomplished, and these are in part our work. True eschatological spirituality isn't to wait and long for the parousia, nor even—as some christians think—to anticipate it, but to hasten it (2 Pet 3 : 12). And the only means revealed to us for doing this is to preach the gospel throughout the world—'and then the end will come' (Mt 24: 14). Thus Christ's coming depends on us!

The end of the world is a continual and a contemporary event. To every generation a world crumbles away and a world is born. Every generation has its Antichrist to rally all those who are disappointed in Christ, and to put forward effective measures, organisations without mercy, and powers without love to those who are weary of seeing love without power. Death and resurrection begin with the baptism of each one of us. The judgement is permanent: we are judged at every encounter with our neighbour! (Mt 25:40). The last judgement isn't something new, added to the sum of particular judgements, nor is it a ceremony of handing out decorations and haloes. It is the full and final manifestation of the judgement which is ever active and present, of which it could be said in our Lord's time, 'Now is the judgement of this world' (Jn 12:31).

The parousia will be the revealing of all Christ's work. Thus it, too, is progressive, and will only gradually become full and evident—not suddenly and finally as the 'waiting' school of thought imagine. There will certainly be a fresh intervention by Christ, but we shall not be able to realise its importance in advance, because we don't know to what point we shall, drawn by grace, be raised. That transformation, which will eternalise our work and Christ's merged into one, could be as gentle as a flower opening, as joyous as a butterfly emerging from its chrysalis.

That will be the moment when Christ, having so often leant over the humble bread of this earth, the symbol and fruit of man's labour, to declare that he made it his body, does the same at the end of time for our world, regenerated by his grace and our efforts. He will be able to say, 'Come, and live here for ever. This is my kingdom, at last perfect, which I prepared for you from the beginning of the world.'

Salvation is collective. Salvation is personal, of course. No one will be saved without wanting to, and it will profit us nothing if we have gained the whole world and suffered the loss of our own soul. But it is in no way a contradiction to declare that it is also collective. We are responsible one for another. We shall not enter heaven alone. Anyone concerned only with his own salvation is damned. The fall was collective—which still disturbs us— and the redemption is too; so much so that baptism gives us grace only by incorporating us into a saving group: the church. Can anyone be a catholic and not agonised over making the redemption universal? Do we really need the whole world to be saved—or are we cheerfully resigned to a certain wastage? What is the number of the elect? Is anyone damned, and how many? There was a time when people rejoiced at being among the small number of the elect! Now—and surely everyone would agree that it is an improvement— we have become much more aware of the collective dimension in humanity. We now feel such a strong sense of solidarity that really good people can't feel resigned to the loss of even one of their brothers.

Péguy longed for a city which wouldn't close its gates to a single unfortunate. His only error was in believing that heaven ever closes its gates at all: it is the damned who refuse to go in, and who would be unhappy if they were made to. The existence of hell is indispensable. Otherwise, heaven would be a concentration camp: 'if we're *obliged* to go there, then I'm not going!'—if it's to be free, then one must be able to go elsewhere. Heaven is the place where people love. One can only go to it freely. The existence of hell is the expression of God's respect for our freedom. God will never force anyone to love him, and hell is the refuge of those who refuse to love him. But is hell in fact inhabited? That depends on us. It too is free; and as our freedom is a unity, it depends on us all.

We know nothing of the number of the damned —or even if there are any. The church canonises, assuring us that certain people are saved. But it doesn't damn; we aren't obliged by faith to believe that any specific person is in hell. I have pointed out the ambiguity of the gospel texts on such points as the number of the elect. The redemption is not 'ready-made' but 'in the making'. Its dimensions, its extent, its fulfilment are all still taking shape. They depend on us. The failure of the texts to be precise is an appeal to our freedom. Whether hell be empty or full is not yet determined; the decision rests with mankind as a whole. We are not informed about it because it is we who must make it so. We must believe in the possibility of damnation—and he is naïve indeed who does not feel in himself the reality, and even the attraction, of such a refusal and despair. Forgetfulness of hell or disbelief makes sinners, but faith in hell makes redeemers. Christ knew hell—not the hells of stage or mythology, of Virgil or Dante, but the hell eating away the souls of so many of us; the hell of sterility, of perversity, of boredom driving us to seek distraction, forgetfulness, and even death. To save us from that hell, Jesus was made flesh, spoke, taught, prayed, suffered and was crucified. Our faith in hell will make us redeemers, too.

Each day at mass the church prays *pro totius mundi salute*: for the salvation of the whole world. What can be prayed for can also be hoped for. As long as there are one or two left to pray, to suffer, and to love, we need not despair of giving back to God the whole of this world which he has so loved.